Citizen Participation in Public Decision Making

Citizen Participation in Public Decision Making

EDITED BY

Jack DeSario

AND

Stuart Langton

PREPARED UNDER THE AUSPICES
OF THE POLICY STUDIES
ORGANIZATION

CONTRIBUTIONS IN POLITICAL SCIENCE,
NUMBER 158

Greenwood Press
NEW YORK · WESTPORT, CONNECTICUT · LONDON

Library of Congress Cataloging-in-Publication Data

Citizen participation in public decision making.

(Contributions in political science, ISSN 0147-1066 ;
no. 158)
"Prepared under the auspices of the Policy Studies Organization."
Bibliography: p.
Includes index.
1. Political participation—United States.
2. Technocracy. I. DeSario, Jack. II. Langton, Stuart.
III. Policy Studies Organization. IV. Series.
JK1764.C525   1987   323'.042'0973   86-7571
ISBN 0-313-25478-8 (lib. bdg. : alk. paper)

Library of Congress Catalog Card Number: 86-7571
ISBN: 0-313-25478-8
ISSN: 0147-1066

First published in 1987

Greenwood Press, Inc.
88 Post Road West, Westport, Connecticut 06881

Printed in the United States of America

∞

The paper used in this book complies with the
Permanent Paper Standard issued by the National
Information Standards Organization (Z39.48-1984).

10 9 8 7 6 5 4 3 2 1

Contents

Contents

Figures and Tables

Preface

The role of government has expanded dramatically over the past few decades in providing to the general public essential domestic services such as health care, educational programs, a clean environment, and efficient transportation networks. These increased governmental responsibilities have led to a concomitant growth of a large and "expert" public decision-making process at the national, state, and local levels. This process is of increasing importance to society because of its many important responsibilities, such as (1) the setting of public standards (examples may include determining air and water pollution standards, acceptable workplace conditions, and the appropriate supply and distribution of medical facilities); (2) the organization of current health, education, and housing systems; (3) the allocation of public finances to worthy public programs; (4) planning for future domestic programs for many policy areas.

Traditionally, these important decisions were made by public bureaucrats who possessed a high degree of technical expertise but who were not directly accountable to the citizens of the affected localities or states. Recently, many citizen reform groups throughout the nation have expressed their dissatisfaction with the outcomes of this expert or technocratic administrative process and have called for more public accountability through the direct inclusion of citizen members in local and state agencies.

Government has responded at all levels by trying to establish a new generation of public decision making that incorporates both citizens and experts (democratic versus technocratic models). Consumer membership mandated by state and national legislation has witnessed the incorporation of citizens in many important health, education, transportation, and environmental planning bodies. This innovative merger and its impact on formulating, directing, and implementing public policies has assumed great importance in light of the expanded role of government and the advent of the technological era. New technological capabilities and applications have profound implications for almost every aspect of society. Never before has mankind had the imminent capability to achieve such radical constructive and destructive alterations of society. The purpose of this volume is to evaluate the adequacy and contributions of current decision-making bodies for a diversity of policy areas, such as education, health, environment, transportation, and housing. Based upon this analysis, recommendations on how to optimize the contributions of experts and citizens will be formulated.

This topic is organized into three major sections. The introductory segment considers the major theoretical and normative implications of a decision-making process that includes experts and/or citizens. Issues of particular importance to be addressed are:

1. What are the benefits and detriments of having citizens involved in public decision making?
2. What are the benefits and detriments of leaving public decision making to experts?
3. What are the problems inherent in devising a public decision-making system that includes both citizens and experts?
4. What are the problems of citizen involvement in light of enduring and growing restrictions imposed by increasing technological complexity and high technology?

The second section analyzes several specific policy areas (health, education, and environment) to determine the actual contributions of citizens in the formulation of policies. Issues of major concern within this section include:

1. What kinds of citizens are involved in directing these public programs?
2. What difference does it make if citizen members to planning boards do or do not reflect the same demographic background as the general community?
3. What are the relative contributions of citizen versus expert groups in this public process?

The final section considers the future of citizen participation. A theoretical framework is devised which explains the various decision-making processes utilized across policy areas and helps to explain what the optimal contributions of technocrats and citizens may be within particular social contexts. This section will detail suggestions for optimizing the contributions of the technocratic and democratic models both as an administrative and communicative process.

A number of individuals and organizations have provided the help and intellectual assistance necessary to the completion of this project. We are grateful to the Kettering Foundation and the Gund Foundation for their financial aid which allowed us to host a conference organized around this theme. This conference provided intellectual interaction and evolution essential to this volume. We would like to thank the Lincoln Filene Center for Citizenship and Public Affairs at Tufts University for their institutional support and encouragement. We are grateful to the Dean's Office of Western Reserve College, Case Western Reserve University for office space and additional funds for communications and administration. We wish to thank all our contributors whose enthusiasm, patience, and intelligence were essential to the successful completion of this project. We would like to thank Sharon Skowronski for her typing, editorial, budgetary, and general organization skills which insured the efficient and effective completion of this project. We would also like to recognize the assistance of Vincent E. McHale, Chairman of the Political Science Department at Case Western Reserve University for his continual support and encouragement. Finally, we would like to thank Dennis Palumbo, the Editor-in-Chief of the *Policy Studies Review*, and Stuart Nagel, the Secretary-Treasurer of the Policy Studies Organization, for recognizing the importance of this topic and allowing us to draw upon their excellent reputations and those of their organizations to promote this project in its initial stage.

Part I

DEMOCRACY AND TECHNOCRACY: AN OVERVIEW

1

Citizen Participation and Technocracy

JACK DESARIO AND STUART LANGTON

"The most revolutionary and cataclysmic event in the history of the world is the emergence of technological knowledge," observed philosopher Nicholas Berdyaev over thirty years ago. Since then, the profound impact of technology has become even more visible as we recognize that "three-quarters of all scientists who have ever lived are now alive and [that] the doubling rate of knowledge has been reduced from millennia to around a decade" (Moore, 1972). Today the exponential growth of technological knowledge is found in fields as diverse as communications, medicine, weaponry, agricultural data handling, and chemistry. The rate of change that accompanies this quantum leap in technological knowledge is so accelerated, as John Platt (1969) points out, that it can be described as ten Industrial Revolutions and Protestant Revolutions combined and occurring in a single generation.

What impact have these transformations had on our lives? New technological capabilities and applications have been found to bear profound implications for almost every aspect of society. In the workplace, our transitions from an industrial to what has alternatively been referred to as the postindustrial, service, or informational economy has created a need for new occupational skills and resources (Bell, 1973; Naisbitt, 1982). Domestic life has been altered by changes in the role, structure, and proximity of the family. General environmental conditions are being seriously threatened, both directly and indirectly, by our interventions. Direct threats now abound through the new-found omnipotence of our technology (nuclear power, DDT, recombinant DNA), and indirect threats result as a by-product of the changing energy consumption needs that they generate. Even our secular and nonsecular attitudes have been modified by the challenges of the technological specter.

Never before has mankind had the imminent capability to achieve such radical constructive and destructive alterations of society. If technology is viewed as instrumental, it is important to identify the social mechanisms and values which direct and organize this knowledge. The pervasiveness of our current capabilities enhances the significance of calculated social planning.

James Wallace (1979) reminds us that our society does not have to be a "helpless spectator" and that technological capability should not always be equated with technological desirability. The doctrine of *laissez-innover* has been widely rejected by most commentators and citizens as the sole principle of development. However, the problem of "restructuring our decision-making mechanisms—including the system of market incentives—so that the increasing number and importance of social issues that confront us can be resolved equitably and effectively" has been the subject of widespread disagreement and debate (Mesthene, 1981). In other words, even if we accept the principle of planned social change, we are still confronted with the chore of having to determine the types of decision-making processes that should be entrusted with this important task. The following passage from a report by the President's Commission for a National Agenda for the Eighties conveys the sense of urgency and the parameters involved in constructing an effective decision-making approach.

The nation . . . may be at a crucial point in its history; technological complexity and ability to regulate may no longer be in balance. If so, our decision-making processes need to be critically examined to determine whether they are adequate for future challenges. The national agenda for the next decade should include consideration of mechanisms consistent with a democratic society that permits public participation in decisions that potentially could affect the lives of many people—the uses of scientific and technical knowledge. During the decade of the eighties, our social needs to examine critically the relationship between scientific expertise and democratic policy making . . . the management of increasing scientific and technological complexity poses a difficult challenge for public and private institutions, requiring flexibility and adjustment at all levels. . . . However, a nascent contradiction may exist between the requisites of science and the requisites of democracy. (1980:3)

Technocracy and democracy have clearly emerged as the chief protagonists in technological struggles. The purpose of this book is to provide a better understanding of the contributions, biases, and interrelationships between these two social forces. These concepts have illicited a wide array of images and definitions. As a result of our focused interest in current public decision-making bodies, we have opted for very specific applications of these terms. Technocracy, for our purposes, is the application of technical knowledge, expertise, techniques, and methods to problem solving, while democracy is used to refer to citizen involvement activities in relation to government planning and policy making.

TECHNOCRATIC DECISION MAKING

In recognition of the social importance of modern technologies, the federal government has acquired a central role in the development, application, and regulation of those technologies. The methods of public policy making that government has employed to accomplish this task have varied considerably over the decades. Initial postwar interventions were closely monitored by Congress. During the 1950s and 1960s, however, as the scope and implications of technology increased, the ability of our legislature to evaluate these innovations was greatly diminished. How could legislators be expected to comprehend the obscure side effects and specialized formulae for a host of technologies that were developing in areas such as agriculture, energy, transportation, medicine, and electronics?

The optimism of the era seemed to provide a logical solution to this dilemma. Concerted efforts on the part of the government were believed to have the capability to solve even the most perplexing challenges of our universe. After all, the mysteries of the atom were successfully solved and our large commitments to NASA and the space program promised to conquer the "new frontier." The solution to national public policy making was simply a national commitment to mobilize the resources and cadres of experts necessary for the rational scientific approach. David Collingridge, noting the enthusiasm engendered by these initial successes, captured the spirit of the time when he wrote:

These successes engendered great optimism about the future benefits obtainable from technology. . . . The horizon seemed limitless—all that was required was the organization, the skill, the dedication, the tenacity, and the willingness to invest in success so characteristic of these great triumphs, and there surely could be no barriers to technology satisfying almost any known purpose. All that could stand in the way of curing disease, prolonging life, feeding the hungry, providing an abundance of energy, giving wealth to the poor, was lack of will and organization. (1980:13)

This logic and optimism associated with the gathering of knowledge by experts led to the development of "new complexes of techno-political direction" such as planning units, advisory commissions, study and policy groups, and regulatory agencies whose manifest mission was "to provide knowledge and political acumen for control over the many related industrial, distributional, and service complexes that had evolved" (LaPorte and Abrams, 1976:36–37). A large, specialized, professional bureaucracy was quickly assembled. The number of scientists employed by the federal government increased by 49 percent from 1960 to 1970 while the number of social scientists increased by 52 percent (Nelkin, 1981:295). By the early 1960s, the proportion of professional-type positions in the federal bureaucracy exceeded 50 percent. As the decade progressed, professional bureaucracies grew in size and importance. Administrative agencies were increasingly delegated the political authority to determine public standards; to organize health, education, transportation, and housing systems; to allocate finances to worthy public programs; and to plan future programs for a diversity of domestic policy areas. The federal bureaucracy currently "issues approximately 7,000 rules and policy statements a year, 2,000 of which legally bind the citizenry" (Carter, 1983:15).

Private-sector organizations have simultaneously experienced a parallel growth in the numbers and influence of experts. The most rapidly growing proportion of employees in corporations consists of scientists, engineers, and technologists. From 1950 to 1965, the "number of scientists and engineers in the United States increased five times faster than the population" (Berkley, 1981:475). John Kenneth Galbraith and others have noted that our private organizations are increasingly being run by a new "technostructure." This technostructure "embraces all who bring specialized knowledge, talent, or experience to group decision making" (Galbraith, 1967:71).

The expert has clearly become an integral part of our decision-making bodies in both the public and private sectors. This trend has been viewed with alarm by many because these professional cadres operate almost independently of democratic processes. Is this large delegation of power and discretion warranted? To provide some insight into the expert's adequacy as social engineer, we must determine who these experts are and what special competencies they possess.

CHALLENGES TO TECHNOCRACY

Experts are conferred a special status by their peers after they demonstrate a mastery over a technique and/or body of knowledge. The training they receive, including a familiarity with the "theories, models, procedures, and formulas of science and technology," has generally led us to believe that one trained in the use of these scientific tools has the ability to "calculate an unambiguously correct answer" (Mazur, 1973:25). In addition to their precision, technocrats are seen as being imbued with social objectivity and neutrality.

Recent applications and experiences have cast doubt upon many of these assumptions. It has been found that scientific

and technocratic approaches have "not only failed to solve social problems but often contributed to them" (Nelkin, 1981:274).
The "moon-ghetto" metaphor is frequently recited within this
context to symbolize the variety of complaints levied at the
shortcomings of technocratic decision making. Simply stated, it
asks: "If we can land a man on the moon, why can't we solve
the problems of the ghetto?" (Nelson, 1974:376). Social failures
such as these have precipitated an extensive array of methodological and normative critiques of the technocratic model. These
analyses and the dialogue they provoke provide understanding
of the potentials and limitations of expert decision making.

Many of the problems of technocracy emerged only after these
techniques were applied to social problems and issues. This
pattern is not coincidental. The methodologies of experts are
most effective when considering technical decisions versus value,
or mixed, decisions. Technical decisions require the application
and extrapolation of science to determine and harness the potential of "what is." Value questions involve normative determinations of "what should be." Scientific information may provide useful guidance for deciding value questions; however, it
is rarely the sole determinant. The production of industrial ro-
bots or atom bombs were technical problems that were successfully mastered by scientific methods. The question of whether
and how we should deploy these technical wonders are value
issues over which scientists may have no particular provi-
dence.

The problem for experts is that the issues they most frequently confront when addressing social problems are "mixed
decisions"—involving both technical and value judgments
(Kantrowitz, 1975:506). Therefore, the performance of technocracy in the social sphere is a success only if it can satisfy both
components of the issue. David Collingridge provides an illus-
trative example of this premise when he compares the great
successes of the Manhattan Project and the moon landing to
the perceived failures of the Green Revolution:

The difference between the success and failure in no way stems from
a technical miscalculation on the part of technologists. The key difference here is that the objectives given to the successful programs were

purely technical. Success for the Manhattan Project was a bomb which exploded with more than a particular force. Success for the moon program was the landing of a piece of hardware carrying a man and its safe return to Earth. The Green Revolution is quite different. Its objective was not a technical one, but a human one. The revolution's aim was not [just] the breeding of high yielding cereals, but the bringing of food to the very poor. The Green Revolution is highly successful in the sense of its technical achievement but a total failure because these vast efforts have all been in quite the wrong direction. The lesson from this is salutary: our understanding of the physical and biological world in which we live is extremely deep, and provides us with means for the production of all kinds of technical marvels; but our appreciation of how these marvels effect society is perilous. (1980:15)

Expanding on this theme, the successful application of technocratic decision making to social problems is perilous for two major reasons. First, social issues are less adequately understood, precise, and measurable (scientifically) than technical concerns. Second, expert decision-making bodies must also confront the highly emotional normative considerations that require the effective translation of social values and objectives into public policies. Experts' exact responsibilities and contributions to goal development is the subject of increased contention.

The "hard science" associated with the technical decisions such as physics, biology, and engineering are characterized by precise and well-developed theories that are firmly established by empirical verification. Determinations within these fields do not invoke value questions; rather they are based upon deductive logic and formulae. Methodological techniques applied to social issues are increasingly referred to as the "soft sciences" because they are not characterized by the same rigor as those of the hard sciences. The Brooks Report, which reviews social decision-making capabilities, claims that "the conditions for the success achieved in many space and defense projects are not yet evident in the social sphere" (OECD, 1971:56). Specifically, social goals are complex, conflicting, and unclear. Theoretical knowledge and models of society are incomplete and inconsistent, and there is little agreement over what our objectives should be.

Science is most effective in achieving objectives, not in defining them. Given the initial realities of social problems, the deficiencies of technocratic applications are obvious. Expert social analysis places a great deal of faith in the "logic of choice drawn from economics, statistical decision theory, and operations research to aid in decision making in a way regarded as ethically neutral. But the logic of choice depends on prior specification of objectives, or agreement about the nature of relevant benefits and costs. Only after these objectives are agreed upon is it possible to pose the problems of choice in a technical and neutral way" (Nelson, 1974:380–81). We have already indicated that social objectives are not well defined. So how do technocrats make decisions? Does their approach most effectively promote the best programs and the goals of our society?

Evaluations of cost-benefit techniques utilized by public decision-making bodies provide a good example of the measurement problems and implied normative biases of the soft sciences. Cost-benefit analysis is widely used throughout our professional bureaucracies to clarify objectively the most effective program among all social programs. The merits of a program, according to this technique, can be determined by adding up the costs and benefits of each and choosing the program with the higher excess of benefits over costs. Technical problems arise due to an inability to estimate the cost and/or benefits of many social programs. For many policies, such as cancer research, it is impossible to know the actual costs of goal achievement. Estimating benefits is difficult because, in most cases, market prices do not exist for social programs. In the absence of market price, policies are compared by "computing the present value of the income increase that would be attributable to each and determining which promises the highest rate of return on the last dollar invested" (Rivlin, 1971:52).

The utilization of the present value of income criteria in turn raises many questions about the purported neutrality of this technique. Estimated present value of additional income would logically be higher for men and highly educated groups because of their greater earning potential. This decision-making method would, therefore, objectively favor programs that benefit higher-status groups. This criterion also assumes the "acceptance of an increase in the national income as an overriding goal. It implies that this goal is more important than good health or better education or the elimination of poverty, and that these goals are legitimate only to the extent that they increase future income" (Rivlin, 1971:56–57).

The objectivity and precision of expert decision making is not as compelling to the public when it becomes aware of these measurement and value biases. Policy experts, as a result of their methodological orientation, are increasingly seen as stressing rational efficiency standards, which are often "insensitive to and/or incompatible with the goal of humane democratic government. The lens of the specialist is not necessarily the lens of the humanist" (Morrow, 1975:181).

Many observers are also concerned that the recommendations of experts in regard to these important "mixed decisions" may be influenced by personal values rather than technical feasibility. Kantrowitz warns that it is inevitable "that scientists who have been engaged in research relevant to the scientific side of great mixed decisions should have deeply held political and moral positions on the relationship of their work to society" (1975:506). This contention illustrates the difficulty of attempting to isolate the technical versus value components of a mixed decision. How do we know when an expert's evaluation of an issue reflects his or her scientific opinion or his or her normative preferences?

TECHNOLOGICAL SKEPTICISM AND CITIZEN PARTICIPATION

While many people still retain a naive faith in experts and technological progress, a growing proportion of Americans has become more skeptical of technology and its elite. For example, between 1966 and 1976 the percentage of the public expressing a great deal of confidence in the scientific community declined from 56 to 43 percent (Nelkin, 1981:273) and a 1979 survey indicated that 42 percent of the public believed that "you can't trust what experts like scientists and technical people say because often what they say isn't right" (National Science Board, 1981:176).

One significant result of such growing skepticism is a heightened demand for greater citizen participation in regard to technological decisions. To be sure, the rapidly growing interest in increased participation in our society is not solely associated with technological issues. In part, at least, as John Naisbitt (1982) has pointed out, greater demands for participation by workers, consumers, and citizens is one of the great megatrends of our time. The dramatic growth of government-sponsored citizen involvement requirements and programs since the adoption of the Administrative Procedures Act in 1946 has been described by Langton (1981). A corresponding growth of grass-roots citizen activism has also taken place during the same time as evidenced by the emergence of over twenty social movements and the powerful impact of interest groups on American politics (Langton, 1978).

What is particularly significant about the rise of technology and citizen participation during the postwar years is that these two separate revolutionary trends have continued on relatively parallel paths while seldom intersecting. Prior to 1970, for example, citizen participation was primarily organized around social issues, such as welfare, housing, civil rights, and education, as citizens seemed content to let experts handle other, more complex, technological matters. However, since the rise of the environmental and consumer movements in the early 1970s, there has been a growing convergence between citizen participation and the technological establishment. As the public has become more uneasy about the impacts of technology and the power of experts, citizens and many of their representatives have demanded greater participation in dealing with complex technological issues, such as the management of air and water quality, control of hazardous wastes, nuclear power, and recombinant DNA research. One example of this, as Walter Rosenbaum (1979) has noted, is that the greatest number of federal public participation requirments established during the 1970s included issues of this sort.

Coincidentally, citizen interest groups have discovered that many technological policy issues previously ignored or delegated to experts have a substantial influence on their particular interests. As a result, in the last decade there has been a rise in scientific research, public education, and advocacy activities among citizen interest groups in regard to technological issues. So, for example, labor unions have taken the initiative in examining health hazards arising from carcinogenic substances in the workplace; the elderly are concerned about complex health policy issues concerning CAT scanners, kidney dialysis, and organ transplants; and gay persons have mobilized over federal research policies concerning AIDS.

All of this portends a significant alteration in the technological and citizen participation revolutions as the two intersect more frequently in the future. So-called technological progress will be increasingly challenged by the forces of democratic examination as the shortcomings of technological methods and experts become more publicized and citizen activism over technological issues will grow as citizen organizations discover and share their ability to examine and influence policy over such issues. Further, heightened citizen participation is a force waiting to explode in relation to a host of troublesome technological issues in the wings of the public policy arena. For example, such issues as the influence of the robotics industry on employment patterns, the potential dangers of low-level radiation from high-technology machinery in the workplace, and the possible development of "star wars" military satellites involve technological issues that are bound to stir considerable public action.

These forces suggest that the practices and traditions of technological development and citizen participation are being altered dramatically. No longer can technocrats proceed without regard to public scrutiny and influence. No longer can concerned citizens and their organizations ignore or delegate technological matters to the high priests of technology. Consequently, technologists will have to develop their soft skills in relation to the public, while citizen organizations will have to perfect their capacity to confront the hard issues of technology. No longer will the two be able to live in isolation from one another.

TOWARD A TECHNODEMOCRATIC SOCIETY

The extent to which technological development and citizen participation can interact and coexist in harmony is a very open question. We do not know with any degree of certainty if technology is susceptible to public control or if citizens are capable of sufficient interest and understanding to impact thoughtfully on technological decisions. Further, we are far from clear on matters of what kinds of structures and procedures would be necessary to develop and maintain a healthy "technodemo-cratic" society. Nonetheless, for better or worse, the weight of historical momentum is pressing us to experiment and create a technodemocracy that can combine the values of technological growth, individual freedom and influence, and enlightened regulation in the public interest.

There are many observers who are far from optimistic about such a possibility. A number of critics have warned of potential social catastrophe as a consequence of technological power (Forrester, 1971; Ellul, 1964; Heilbroner, 1974). Some have raised doubts about the level of civic interest and ability of our citizens (Sennett, 1974; Lasch, 1979); others have worried that increased citizen participation will lead to political instability and disruption (Huntington, 1974).

To add to such pessimistic assessments, it should be acknowledged that our recent national experience in regulating technology has been checkered and replete with horror stories (for example, Love Canal, Three Mile Island, Toxic Shock Syndrome, Agent Orange, and Acid Rain). At the same time, our experiences with citizen participation have been wanting in many respects. Despite hundreds of federal regulations for public involvement programs and the expenditure of millions of dollars, the most common participation procedures, such as public hearings and advisory committees, are more often the most wasteful and useless. Further, the rise of interest group advocacy all too frequently contributes to an adversary political culture which inhibits consensus.

Despite sobering predictions, observations, and experience, the challenge of relating technocracy and democracy remains. While acknowledging the difficulties of such a task, it should also be noted that it is one that has not received substantial understanding and commitment. In this regard, we find the judgment of G. Bingham Powell, Jr., to be most instructive in noting that "the capacities of citizens to learn and the capacities of leaders to lead and devise new, democratic arrangements for citizen involvement and organized control have been too little tried to justify . . . a pessimistic prediction" (1982:28).

This collection of essays is inspired by such an experimental attitude toward the development of citizen participation in regard to technological decision making. As such it rejects both romantic and hostile postures toward technology. While we can appreciate the attempts of some individuals to retreat from the rigors of a technocratic society, such an option is impossible as a matter of public policy. As Berdyaev (1959) has observed, "a return from the life which is technically organized to the life which is naturally organic is an impossibility." Further, a neo-Luddite position strikes us as an attitude of hostile desperation which has as much value as cursing the darkness. The problem of technology, as Geoffrey Vickers (1972) has pointed out, is not technology per se but the extent to which we have failed to control and guide it according to human values. Therefore, the real and unavoidable problem of technology is one of human community. Lacking at present is the capacity of our people to determine collectively the role, functions, and limits of technology. Quite simply, such determination cannot be achieved without a substantial degree of citizen participation.

The successful adaptation of decision-making processes to increased social and technical complexity has been viewed as one of the most critical concerns of the decade. The relative role posited for democracy and technocracy will have a profound impact upon issues such as the efficacy, effectiveness, and responsiveness of public policies. Hopefully, the efforts of our contributors will provide some insights into these issues and will serve as the impetus for more rigorous and systematic thought about how best to promote the values of our society.

REFERENCES

Bell, Daniel 1973
    The Coming of Post-Industrial Society. (New York: Basic Books).
Berdyaev, Nicholas 1959
    The Beginning and the End. (New York: Harper and Bros.).
Berkley, George 1983
    The Craft of Public Administration. (Boston: Allyn and Bacon).

Carter, Lief 1983

> *Administrative Law and Politics.* (Boston: Little, Brown).

Collingridge, David 1980

> *The Social Control of Technology.* (New York: St. Martin's Press).

Ellul, Jacques 1964

> *The Technological Society.* (New York: Vintage Books).

Forrester, Jay 1971

> *World Dynamics.* (Cambridge, Mass.: Wright Allen Press).

Galbraith, John Kenneth 1967

> *The New Industrial State.* (Boston: Houghton Mifflin).

Heilbroner, Robert 1974

> *An Inquiry into the Human Prospect.* (New York: W. W. Norton).

Huntington, Samuel P. 1974

> "Postindustrial Politics: How Benign Will It Be?" *Comparative Politics* 6:163–91.

Kantrowitz, Arthur 1975

> "Controlling Technology Democratically," *American Scientist* 63:505–9.

Langton, Stuart 1978

> *Citizen Participation in America.* (Lexington, Mass.: Lexington Books).

——— 1981

> "Evolution of a Federal Citizen Involvement Policy," *Policy Studies Review* 1:369–78.

LaPorte, Todd, and C. Abrams 1976

> "Alternative Patterns of Postindustria," in Leon Lindberg, ed., *Politics and the Future of Postindustrial Society.* (New York: David McKay).

Lasch, Christopher 1979

> *The Culture of Narcissism.* (New York: W. W. Norton).

Mazur, Allan 1973

> "Disputes Between Experts," *Minerva* 10:244–62.

Mesthene, Emmanuel 1981

> "The Role of Technology in Society," in Albert Teich, ed., *Technology and Man's Future,* 3d ed. (New York: St. Martin's Press).

Moore, Wilbert, ed. 1972

> *Technology and Social Change.* (Chicago: Quadrangle Books).

Morrow, William 1975

> *Public Administration.* (New York: Random House).

Naisbitt, John 1982

> *Megatrends.* (New York: Warner Books).

National Science Board 1981
    Science Indicators. (Washington, D.C.: Government Printing Office).
Nelkin, Dorothy 1981
    "Science and Technology Policy and the Democratic Process," in Albert Teich, ed., *Technology and Man's Future*, 3d ed. (New York: St. Martin's Press).
Nelson, Richard 1974
    "Intellectualizing About the Moon-Ghetto Metaphor," *Policy Sciences* 5:275–314.
OECD 1971
    Science, Growth, and Society. (Paris, France: OECD).
Platt, John 1969
    "What We Must Do," *Science* 166:1115–21.
Powell, G. Binghman, Jr. 1982
    "Social Progress and Liberal Democracy," in G. Almond, M. Chodorow, and R. H. Pearce, eds., *Progress and Its Discontents*. (Berkeley: University of California Press).
President's Commission for a National Agenda for the Eighties 1980
    Science and Technology Promises and Dangers in the Eighties. (Washington, D.C.: Government Printing Office).
Rivlin, Alice 1971
    Systematic Thinking for Social Action. (Washington, D.C.: Brookings Institution).
Rosenbaum, Walter 1979
    "Public Participation: Required, But Is It Important?" *Citizen Participation* 1:1–12.
Sennett, Richard 1974
    The Fall of Public Man. (New York: Knopf).
Vickers, Geoffrey 1972
    Freedom in a Rocking Boat: Changing Values in an Unstable Society. (Middlesex, England: Penguin Books).
Wallace, James 1979
    "Freedom and Direction," in John Burke and Marshall Eakin, ed., *Technology and Change*. (San Francisco: Boyd and Fraser).

2

The Politics of Policy Analysis: The Role of Citizen Participation in Analytic Decision Making

MARY GRISEZ KWEIT AND ROBERT W. KWEIT

It seems clear that the United States is entrenched in a period where the dominant characteristic of the political environment is scarcity. Unlike the politics of the Great Society in the 1960s, in which the major political question concerned the relative size of the piece of pie allocated to various programs, the major question of the 1980s has become which programs will receive no part of the pie at all. Among the impacts of such a politics of scarcity is a greater emphasis on the rationality of decisions. To achieve this, greater use will likely be made of policy analytic techniques.

Ironically, the use of policy analysis began as a major innovation in the 1960s. In the midst of affluence the belief was widespread that policy could be designed to allocate resources as rationally as possible. While policy analysis may have been born in affluence, it is even more relevant to an environment of scarcity. There are two reasons why scarcity leads to an emphasis on rationality and analytic techniques aimed at achieving rational policy. First, the more limited the resources, the more crucial it becomes to allocate those resources in ways to produce the maximum amount of benefit. Waste is not tolerable unless resources are infinite, or at least abundant. A second, less obvious, reason why rationality may become more important in periods of scarcity is the increasing need to justify programs to budgetary officials in the legislative and executive branches.

It may appear that the expanding use of policy analytic techniques and the greater emphasis on rationality would have negative impacts on citizen participation in the policy process. When the emphasis is placed on rationality, it may appear that there is no role for participation. However, it shall be shown that there is no necessary contradiction between rational policy produced by policy analysis and the use of citizen participation in the policy process. This chapter will focus on why and how participation can play a role in rational policy making. Before turning to this, the reasons for the expansion of policy analysis and the apparent conflict between policy analysis and citizen participation must be examined.

POLICY ANALYSIS AND CITIZEN PARTICIPATION

The characteristics of rational decision-making techniques are especially useful as a means to defend policy funding. Such techniques depend initially on the construction of a model as a basis of structuring the essential elements of a particular policy area. Once such a model is constructed and certain basic assumptions are accepted, the outcome of the analysis becomes virtually foreordained by the internal logic. For example, in a benefit-cost analysis, the identification and valuation of the crucial impacts of a policy and the acceptance of the goal of maximizing net benefits leads inevitably to a decision. In a decision analysis, the identification and sequencing of alternative branches of a decision tree and the assignment of payoffs and probabilities will also, from a technocratic perspective, produce a preferred decision once the tree is folded back. The logic of the analysis appears to make the resulting decision inevitable. It appears as though rational man, by the process of right reason, would always reach the same foreordained result. Such an impression, of course, can be very useful in budgetary battles.

A second characteristic of policy analytic techniques, which can be very useful in budgetary battles, is the use of quantification. Numbers seem to give extra legitimacy to arguments, making points somehow more concrete and less debatable. The impact of numbers can be especially strong on those who are unfamiliar with quantitative analysis and who tend to develop symptoms of mathematical anxiety when confronted with tables, charts, and equations.

In general, both the internal logic of the analytic techniques and the use of quantification combine to make the decision reached appear to be inviolate. But there are other ways that policy analysis can be useful to a beleaguered official attempting to defend his or her policy turf. The techniques themselves are not necessarily universally familiar to all those charged with the responsibility for making decisions concerning resource allocation. Especially at state and local levels and among legislative personnel, the awareness of analytic techniques is highly variable. The awe of the unfamiliar and the unwillingness to admit ignorance may be adequate for some to attempt to avoid confrontation with bureaucrats bearing a budgetary request supported by policy analysis. One means of avoidance, of course, is accession to the request. In addition, the single fact that the analysis was done at all may be taken as an indicator of the recognition of and concern for the importance of thrift, thus increasing the credibility of the budgetary request.

There is every reason to believe that the use of policy analytic techniques will increase. Such techniques only appear to serve the goal of allocating scarce resources more effectively and efficiently; their internal logic, quantification, and unfamiliarity tend to create an aura of inviolability to policy proposals, thus helping bureaucrats to defend policy turf during periods of threat.[1]

Policy analysis tends to centralize power in the hands of experts. The use of policy analysis is compatible with bureaucratic decision making, which in many ways is antithetical to citizen participation. Weber's ideal bureaucracy relies on expertise as a means to achieve efficiency. Expertise is also an inherent component of policy analysis since the techniques are specialized enough to be accessible only to experts. Hierarchy, therefore, is a crucial component of the ideal bureaucracy, and to achieve the consensus on goals and values necessary for policy analysis.

In the ideal bureaucracy, there is no place for citizen participation. Citizens will often lack technical expertise, will almost certainly be unfamiliar with bureaucratic routines, and will probably be emotionally involved in issues of concern, rather than being detached and rational. Citizens are outside the hierarchy and therefore hard to control. As a consequence, participation may increase the level of conflict and the time needed to reach decisions. The end result may hamper the efficiency and rationality sought in the ideal bureaucracy and through the use of policy analysis.

As opposed to bureaucratic decision making, democratic decision making is based on the assumption that all who are affected by a given decision have the right to participate in the making of that decision, either directly as in classical democracy or through spokespersons for their point of view in a pluralist-republican model. Such a policy process would have to be nonhierarchical to facilitate access to all those affected. It would also imply no special or dominant role for experts. The criteria for evaluating policy in a democratic process are the accessibility of the process and/or the responsiveness of the policy to those who are affected by it, rather than efficiency or rationality of the decision.

It appears as though we are on the horns of a dilemma. It would seem that it is necessary to choose between rational, efficient policy, which would obviate a role for citizens, and policy which is open and responsive but which is irrational and inefficient. The argument made here, however, is that the Scylla and Charybdis of rational policy versus democratic policy may well be overstated. While policy analytic techniques may create an aura of inviolability for policy, there is no necessary contradiction between the use of those techniques and the involvement of citizens in the policy process. In fact, the case will be made here that citizen input actually may be an important and integral component of the policy analytic techniques most commonly used and, in addition, is inherent in the rational model of policy making.

RATIONAL POLICY MAKING

The fundamental model of rational decision making usually is described as having five steps. First, a problem area must be identified. Second, goals and priorities must be specified. Third, all alternative courses of action are listed and the potential impacts of each are identified. Fourth, some decision criteria or some decision rules are adopted. Finally, a decision is made which maximizes the attainment of the goals.

Many have pointed to the fundamental irrelevance of this model as a guide for actual decision making because of the sheer impossibility of performing most of the steps. While it may sound absurdly easy, identifying a problem area may not actually be so easy. It may be possible to know some problem exists, but to get beyond the vague statement that "something's happening" and to specify clearly what is happening is difficult. Consider the difficulty of identifying precisely what the problem with the economy is.

Goals, again, would seem to be obvious. But once one moves from such general goals as peace and prosperity to more precise and operational goals, problems arise. Where one wants to end up is intimately connected to what one sees as a problem. If the problem with the economy is perceived to be too much government spending, then the goal toward which one aims is a reduction in that spending. On the other hand, if the problem is believed to be the crumbling of the physical plants of industry, then the goal may be expanded governmental involvement in renewal of those physical plants.

A comprehensive listing of all possible alternative routes to achieve the goals is hampered not only by the inability to determine what the problem is and what the goal is but also by the absence of a crystal ball to enable decision makers to see into the future.

The choice of decision criteria on decision rules is also difficult. Such rules are far from unimportant since they determine who wins and who loses. Within the last three decades, a major new field of study has developed to investigate the question of how public choices should be made to maximize social welfare. As Mueller explains it, with our emphasis, public choice "focuses on the problems of aggregating individual preferences to *maximize* a social welfare function" (1979:2). Borrowing heavily from economics, public choice researchers often start with Pareto's optimality as a choice of criterion. Yet they recognize the difficulties transferring that criterion from the economic marketplace, where exchanges are voluntary, to the political marketplace. Government decision makers are often forced to trade off the welfare of one person, or group of people, against others, a situation in which the Pareto criterion is not useful. Thus, the selection of choice criteria remains a debatable issue.

For all of the reasons briefly summarized here, a purely rational decision-making process is impossible. There is, however, a significant way that citizen participation can aid in the process of performing rational decision making. The major limitation inherent in many of the difficulties mentioned above is the lack of comprehensive information. Understanding all aspects of a situation, to be able to identify what the core problem is, is in part a problem of information. Assessing what goal is desirable is related fundamentally to the identification of the problem. But comprehensive information is especially crucial in the identification of alternative solutions and the identification and valuation of the impacts expected from those solutions. While comprehensive information cannot solve the problem of choosing decision rules, it could illuminate many problems involved in making that choice. For instance, comprehensive information would identify what trade-offs in the welfare of different groups are implied in the choice of one policy over another. Information would also point to the expected reaction of the affected groups, an issue of some importance in the political world.

As March and Simon (1958:170–71) indicate, organizations exist to establish boundaries of rationality to deal with the inherent limitations of human capability. Yet since organizations develop limited perspectives by the recruitment and training of members, the development of routines, and the selective perception of information, input from sources outside the organization can be valuable, however unwelcome, to augment the information available to decision makers for nonprogrammed decisions. It is the case, therefore, that citizen participation could be an important source of information to decision makers attempting to make rational policy. Input from citizen groups outside the organizational boundaries could help provide more comprehensive information on all aspects of the policy process.

If there is no necessary contradiction between rational policy making and citizen participation, there may be a conflict between participation and the use of policy analytic techniques, which more decision makers are using to attempt to increase the rationality of the decisions made. Yet, despite the problems of complexity and quantification, there are still ways in which participation can be used in policy analytic techniques.

In a democracy, it is the public that determines where it wants to go, and the role of its representatives and bureaucratic staff is to get them there. In other words, *ends* should be chosen democratically even though *means* are chosen technocratically.

PARTICIPATION AND POLICY ANALYSIS

Benefit-cost analysis is in essence an operational version of the rational model of decision making. An introductory text in policy analysis identifies five steps in the use of benefit-cost analysis as follows:

1. The project or projects to be analyzed are identified.
2. All the impacts, both favorable and unfavorable, present and future, on all of society are determined.
3. Values, usually in dollars, are assigned to these impacts. Favorable impacts will be registered as benefits, unfavorable ones as costs.
4. The *net profit* (total benefit minus total cost) is calculated.
5. The choice is made. (Stokey and Zeckhauser, 1978:136).

Because of its similarity to the rational model, many of the same problems which plague rational decision making plague benefit-cost analysis as well. For example, identifying what projects should be analyzed is analogous to the performance of the first three steps of the rational model: identifying the problem, determining the goals, and listing all alternatives means of achieving those goals. In fact, the first step in benefit-cost analysis often goes further than the rational model requiring that from all alternative means some one or a few means have been chosen for more in-depth analysis. In other words, before the first step in benefit-cost analysis can be performed, analysts must have narrowed the field of study to a scope which is manageable.

This narrowing of the scope is crucial to the final solution of the problem because it in essence puts blinders on the analysts. Bachrach and Baratz (1962, 1963) as well as Cobb and Elder (1972) note that one of the most significant issues in any political system is the ability to place concerns on the agenda for consideration. Schattschneider (1960) notes that the way the issue is placed on the agenda is crucial to the outcome. Whether the projects chosen to be analyzed are not potentially the most effective or the most efficient will never become clear from the analysis since the technique focuses attention only on comparing a given set of projects, not on the comparison of those projects to others. The crucial impact of this first step requires that analysts attempt to maximize the information on the problem area, the goals, and the alternative solutions before the choice of those projects to be analyzed is made. The utility of citizen participation is in its provision of such comprehensive information. The first place, then, in which citizen participation can play a role in benefit-cost analysis is in providing analysts with the background information necessary to narrow the scope of analysis.

The second step of a benefit-cost analysis could also be performed more effectively with the provision of information that is as comprehensive as possible. All potential impacts of a project may never be identified, but citizens are often in a better position to foresee how the shoe will pinch than are those who are designing the projects. This is so partially because the addition of more people will, in almost every case, mean the addition of more viewpoints. In addition, analysts who have designed the policy may feel a sense of identification to it, which may mean that potential negative impacts are unconsciously screened out.

The third step of benefit-cost analysis is perhaps the most

misleading. In this step, values, usually dollar values, are assigned to the impacts that have been identified. It is easy to assign some of those dollar values, but many such valuations are proxy measures of things that cannot be adequately valued quantitatively. As Welch and Comer argue, "the seemingly 'hard data' of cost analyses are based on very slippery estimates of the value of everything from human lives to interest rates" (1983:248).

In the absence of a market price for either costs or benefits, the valuation may best be determined by willingness of those affected to pay either to obtain an impact identified as a benefit or to avoid an impact identified as a cost. This does not imply that payment will ever be made, but it does imply that the valuations should be made by consultations with those who will be affected.

Another place where citizen input may be useful in benefit-cost analysis is in the choice of a discount rate. When the impacts of a project occur over a period of time, future impacts must be discounted so their present value can be determined. In essence, the choice of a discount rate is equivalent to developing an indifference map picturing trade-offs between present and future impacts. The amount by which impacts are discounted will, in many cases, determine whether a project is recommended or not.

This is especially the case with government projects. The resources for government projects come from the private sector. Such resources could be put to other uses in the private economy, and thus there is always an opportunity cost involved in taxes used for public projects. This means the investment opportunities available in the private sector can be used to approximate the discount rate. Yet government projects often have low rates of return on the investment and have benefits which extend over long periods of time. A high discount rate will discourage the choice of such projects. In response, many agencies use artificially low discount rates to make their projects appear to be rational choices. If they used the interest rate available in the private sphere, many government projects could not be rationally recommended by a benefit-cost analysis. The choice of discount rate is therefore crucial.

It must be recognized that the discount rate is not only based on acceptable trade-offs between present and future values but also on trade-offs between groups in society. Those who are making enough money to be taxed—and taxed at high levels— are negatively affected by the use of artificially low discount rates, since it is their tax money which will be used for the government projects that have been recommended by the analysis. Those who are not as well off may not be affected, or they may be positively affected by the receipt of benefits from the government project. Thus, the choice of discount rate is relevant not only to the choice of specific projects but also to questions of how large the public sector of society should be compared to the private sector, how much present value we are willing to trade off for future values, and what kind of re-distributional trade-offs we wish to make between the haves and have-nots in society. While the actual choice of the dis-count rate may be too complex for direct citizen input, infor-mation on citizen preferences about such fundamental ques-tions could be useful in the choice of the rate by analysts.

A final way in which citizen input could be useful in benefit-cost analysis is in the choice of decision rule to be used in se-lecting projects. As indicated before, Pareto optimality may be used to eliminate alternatives in which no one is made better off or someone is made worse off, but it cannot be used to choose between projects that involve redistribution of re-sources or between those that benefit different groups. Kaldor (1939) modified the Pareto criterion to argue that changes should be adopted if the net benefits produced are large enough so that those who are losers could be compensated, whether or not such compensation is actually made. Using either Pareto optimality or the Kaldor-Hicks approach, redistributional poli-cies which did not produce a positive net benefit for society would never be undertaken, regardless of the benefits pro-vided to a particular group within that society.

As with the choice of discount rate, this choice of the deci-sion rule has crucial implications for who will benefit and who will lose as a reult of governmental policies. The decision rule is a normative criterion and thus rests upon values rather than upon scientific verification. Such a choice of values should involve the input of citizens.

Although benefit-cost analysis often appears as though the analysis is based on scientific inevitability, it is actually based upon valuations and judgments which are subjective. While quantification may improve the rigor of the decision process, it should not hide the basic subjectivity inherent in any decision process. Subjective evaluations identifying where the shoe pinches and by how much are within the capabilities of citizens, and by supplying such information to analysts, citizens can potentially make the analysis more relevant.

Technocratic methods are tools that seem to limit the role of public participation. Through sophistry, these tools can be used to justify and reify the wishes of a few. On the other hand, these methods provide a means to aggregate the wishes of the many. It is no longer necessary to deal with ad hoc demands in a haphazard framework. Policy analytic techniques provide structures and a calculus by which to organize democratic demands. The process also highlights those pieces of information that bureaucrats need to serve the public better. In other words, analysis structures the information needed.

Besides benefit-cost analysis, a variety of other technocratic techniques could produce democratic results. For instance, information on subjective probabilities and alternative payoffs could be gathered for use in decision analysis. The value of time versus increased taxes to increase a service bureaucracy could be ascertained for use in queuing models. In short, citizen participation can aid the bureaucrat by supplying the subjective parameters and alternatives necessary for complex policy analytic techniques to provide relevant solutions.

In general, citizen participation has a role to play in common policy analytic techniques by supplying decision makers with more comprehensive information on the potential impacts of policies and the valuation of those impacts. Yet to say that there is a role that participation can play is not the same as concluding that it will be given a chance actually to play that role. Whether that role will be played is dependent on finding mechanisms by which citizen participation can be integrated into the analytic process and providing incentives for decision makers to avail themselves of citizen input.

MECHANISMS FOR CITIZEN INPUT

Any mechanism to gather citizen input should be viewed from a benefit-cost perspective. If participation becomes too costly or benefits are seen as minimal, from either the position of the citizen or the bureaucrat, meaningful citizen participation will break down. Thus, ideally, a way must be found to minimize the cost of participation in terms of time and effort for the citizen and the government official, as well as limit rancor that may result from unrequited expectations. At the same time, benefits must be maximized. The benefits that citizens could receive include more satisfactory government policies and the benefits for bureaucrats include a more trusting and committed citizenry.

Two methods frequently used to determine citizen problems and priorities are public meetings and surveys. The advantage of both of these is that they can be very inclusive. All individuals and groups theoretically have the opportunity to provide input. Unfortunately, these processes often do not work as they are designed. Public meetings are often plagued by low attendance. They also may become a forum for a few dissidents who do not represent the community.[2] Questions, problems, and priorities are often fuzzy. While many groups may be represented, each is usually playing an advocacy role, and trade-offs between groups are usually not considered.

Surveys may be more useful in determining what a cross section of the public wants, but surveys, too, may present problems. For one thing, good surveys are relatively costly. In addition, it is often noted that the public does not have clearly developed opinions. Thus, responses may not be well thought out and may not reflect the true feelings of a community. It is for this reason that many disparage direct democracy through interactive computer-cable television systems.

Much research has indicated that citizen organizations, such as advisory boards or committees, are an effective way of structuring citizen input (Kweit and Kweit, 1981). Such ongoing structures are more likely to be integrated easily into the routine of the bureaucratic agencies which are their targets. Members of such ongoing organizations also can develop expertise in the subject and commitment to the participation process, both of which could increase the quality of communication between the technocrat and the citizens. Problems with such boards, however, arise because of the time and effort they require and the tendency for them to be dominated by those of high socioeconomic status.

Two innovative citizen participation procedures have been used successfully to aid bureaucrats. One promising way to use citizens to define problems is through Delbecq's Nominal Group Technique (Delbecq et al., 1975). In this technique, citizen representatives can be brought together and placed in groups. Unlike regular group decision making based on interaction, participants initially work independently. Lower-class, lower-skilled group members are less likely to be intimidated by professionals or other citizens. Rhetoric and personalities play a smaller role (Delbecq and Van de Ven, 1982:514). Individuals working in groups can be asked to list problems. These problems can then be aggregated and organized, and priorities can even be established. This can be accomplished at one meeting or over a period of time. Many studies have noted that the Nominal Group Technique produces higher quantity, quality, and variety of information than traditional "brainstorming" techniques (Medin, 1975:104). Also, it does not pit the bureaucrat against the citizen, and a clearer picture can be gained.

Another technique that aids the bureaucrat to obtain quality and usable information from citizens is the Delphi Technique (Strauss and Zeigler, 1982:35–38). This technique is especially useful for long-term goal setting. Stage one of the process is the use of a questionnaire to ascertain the views of various "experts" or group representatives. These responses are tabulated. In stage two the questionnaires are returned with a notation on the individual responses and the group responses. The individual is asked if he or she wishes to change his or her mind or justify his or her position. The bureaucrat can stop the process here and decide whether to accept the average stand or whether he or she has been convinced by justifications and arguments of some subgroup in the sample. Alternatively, the bureaucrat can feed back the information for continuing rounds. Because respondents remain anonymous and feedback is obtained, the Delphi Technique may help the bureaucrat to determine whether consensus exists. This should not be overstated, however, since dissenters may drop out, anonymity may result in frivolous responses, or some groupthink may occur despite the anonymity (Strauss and Zeigler, 1982:38).

The point is that there are multiple mechanisms available to decision makers to use citizen input in policy analysis. However, there are consistent problems of ensuring that the decision-making structures are representative of the range of interests in society. The process is costly to citizens in many ways—time, effort, confrontation, for example—and there is a consistent tendency for those who are higher in socio-economic status to be more willing to bear the costs.

Officials could use the analytic models to minimize the costs borne by the citizens. The models help decision makers in focusing and clarifying problems. Points of ambiguity are spotlighted. Officials then could more easily clarify the issues for citizens (however the participation is structured), directing attention to specific questions which need to be resolved. This targeting of attention should help minimize the time involved in participation, and the definition of the issues (although an obvious form of potential control) should help minimize the expertise required of citizens. Both of these impacts may help in obtaining more inclusive participation. Yet the question of whether officials will attempt to integrate citizen participation into policy analytic techniques remains.

INCENTIVES AND DISINCENTIVES FOR OFFICIALS

There are some obvious disincentives for officials to try to increase the use of citizen participation. In the firt place, citizen input is costly not only to the citizens; it is equally costly to officials. This is so in part because of the actual time necessary for the process. Officials must define the issues and listen to or read through the citizens' responses. The demands of time are exacerbated by the very increase in information which the participation process provides. Decisions can be more quickly reached if the full complexity of the situation is not thoroughly understood. Sometimes ignorance is bliss.

A second disincentive is also related to the increase in information provided by participation. Among the things about which the officials may become more informed is the extent to which there is disagreement among the citizens on the valuation of potential impacts. Conflicts may become more obvious to both officials and citizens, and Americans, as a whole, tend not to be comfortable in conflict situations (Weissberg, 1974:69). These conflicts notwithstanding, decisions must be made. Once the conflicts become clear to all, it will also be clear what kinds of trade-offs between the conflicting groups have been produced by the decisions. This may well reduce the acceptance of policy.

It would appear, then, that a bureaucrat's life would be much easier if participation were not integrated into policy analysis. Yet, even ignoring the bureaucrat's altruistic desire to produce better policy, there is one major incentive in the current policy environment which may motivate the bureaucrat to utilize citizen input: the very politics of scarcity that is likely to lead to a greater importance of citizen participation. As Wildavsky (1979:65–67) argued, the best "ubiquitous" strategy of a bureau trying to maximize its allocation in budget battles is to find and cultivate a clientele. And, as Selznick (1949:259–61) long ago demonstrated, a good way to develop a clientele is to co-opt citizens by involving them in the decision process. The involvement of citizens may be a risky strategy because of the potential costs, but the potential payoffs in terms of political support for endangered program may be great. It would seem that the best of all possible worlds for a bureaucrat defending an agency request is to be able to sell his or her programs as rationally determined and supported by citizen demands. Wildavsky (1979:70) also notes that no matter how conservative the group, advisory committees always ask for more.

There is one final development in the policy environment

which has implications for the use of citizen participation in the future. A basic component of Reagan's New Federalism is the decentralization of programs. Decentralization could theoretically aid both the citizen and bureaucrat. Decreasing the service area should result in more homogeneous areas, making it easier for bureaucrats to ascertain the desires of the citizens. By the same token, in a homogeneous environment the costs of participation for citizens are also reduced. It should require less time and effort for decisions to be reached, and the process should involve much less conflict. As Bish argues, "When it is necessary to combine individual demands for a public good, the most efficient political unit for articulating the demand is a relatively homogeneous one (1971:49).

It must, however, be recognized that there are trade-offs which may be necessary if decentralization does occur. While decentralization may be efficient in some ways, it may also be inefficient to the extent that it becomes impossible to realize economies of scale. Bish has realized that

a choice must be made between having hundreds of producers, perhaps requiring very high supervision costs, and having fewer producers who may be able to operate at a lower unit cost while not meeting individual preferences as closely as would be the case if each public good were produced for an area optimum for its own requirements. (1971:58)

In addition, there may be problems of equity if a community is unable to support a recognized minimum amount of service. Finally, the elimination of positive externalities from one government to another hampers redistribution.

CONCLUSION

The current movement for citizen participation began in the 1960s in a policy environment very different from that which exists today. In the politics of affluence and the optimism which it spawned, the belief was widespread that policy could and should be both more responsive to the people and more rational. The dominant characteristic of the current environment is scarcity; thus, the emphasis is likely to be more on the rationality of the distribution of resources, implying limited responsiveness. This fact, combined with the advancement in the knowledge of policy analytic techniques, would seem to make citizen participation less important in the policy process.

Yet we have argued that citizen participation can play a role in such a policy environment. When resources are scarce, it becomes much more important to target them where they will do the most good. Policy analytic techniques are designed to do just that. These techniques, while creating the image of scientific inevitability, actually rest upon the unrealistic assumption that analysts have access to comprehensive information about potential impacts of proposed policies and about the valuation of those impacts. Citizen participation could help the analyst maximize the information available in the policy process, thus integrating rationality and responsiveness. Technocracy is not inherently an enemy of democracy but may be a tool to improve representative decision making.

The use of citizen participation will increase the costs of the policy process by increasing the time involved and the potential for conflict. But there are also incentives for policymakers to involve citizens. The development and cultivation of a clientele is a useful device for providing political support for programs in budgetary battles. The involvement of the citizens in the policy process could help in developing such a supportive clientele. Finally, the decentralization of programs under Reagan's New Federalism could facilitate the participation process by reducing the distance between officials and citizens and increasing the homogeneity in the service area.

NOTES

1. We wish to thank Jeffrey K. Lange, Community Involvement Planner, Northeast Ohio Areawide Coordinating Agency for his useful comments in helping us clarify this and several other points throughout the chapter.

2. Jeffrey Lange correctly noted that it may be an unfair burden to

expect citizen participation to be totally representative. It serves to provide information for decision makers and as such need not be considered representative. We would only add that decision makers may not always appreciate the degree to which participation may not be representative.

REFERENCES

Bachrach, Peter, and Morton Baratz 1962
    "Two Faces of Power," *American Political Science Review* 57:947–52.
——— 1963
    "Decisions and Nondecisions: An Analytic Framework," *American Political Science Review* 57:532–42.
Bish, Robert L. 1971
    The Public Economy of Metropolitan Areas. (Chicago: Markham).
Cobb, Roger, and Charles Elder 1972
    Participation in American Politics: The Dynamics of Agenda-Building. (Boston: Allyn and Bacon).
Delbecq, Andre L., Andrew H. Van de Ven, and David H. Gustafson 1975
    Group Techniques for Program Planning. (Glenview, Ill.: Scott, Foresman).
Delbecq, Andre, and Andrew H. Van de Ven 1982
    "A Group Process Model for Problem Identification and Program Planning," in Richard D. Bingham and Marcus E. Ethridge, eds., *Reaching Decisions in Public Policy and Administration.* (New York: Longman).
Kaldor, Nicholas (1939)
    "Foundations of Welfare Economics," *Economics Journal* 49.
Kweit, Mary Grisez, and Robert W. Kweit 1981
    Implementing Citizen Participation in a Bureaucratic Society. (New York: Praeger Special Studies).
Lowi, Theodore 1979
    The End of Liberalism: The Second Republic of the United States, 2d ed. (New York: W. W. Norton).
March, James G., and Herbert A. Simon 1958
    Organizations. (New York: Wiley).
Medin, Myron J. 1975
    "Make Public Participation Produce Results," *American City and County* 90:104.

Mueller, Dennis C. 1979
  Public Choice. (Cambridge, England: Cambridge University Press).
Ostrom, Vincent 1974
  The Intellectual Crisis in American Public Administration, rev. ed.
  (University: University of Alabama Press).
Schattschneider, E. E. 1960
  The Semi-Sovereign People. (New York: Holt, Rinehart, and Winston).
Selznick, Philip 1949
  TVA and the Grassroots: A Study of Politics and Organization.
  (Berkeley: University of California Press).
Stokey, Edith, and Richard Zeckhauser 1978
  A Primer for Policy Analysis. (New York: W. W. Norton).
Strauss, Harlan J., and L. Harmon Zeigler 1982
  "The Delphi Technique and Its Uses in Social Science Research," in Richard D. Bingham and Marcus E. Ethridge, eds.,
  Reaching Decisions in Public Policy and Administration. (New York: Longman).
Weissberg, Robert 1974
  Political Learning, Political Choice and Democratic Citizenship. (Englewood Cliffs, N. J.: Prentice-Hall).
Welch, Susan, and John C. Comer 1983
  Quantitative Methods for Public Administration: Techniques and Applications. (Homewood, Illinois: Dorsey).
Wildavsky, Aaron 1979
  The Politics of the Budgetary Process. 3d ed. (Boston: Little, Brown).

3

Public Service Science Centers: The Michigan Experience

THOMAS L. VAN VALEY AND JAMES C. PETERSEN[1]

> I don't think it done a bit of good for farmers to go to the courts;
> I think we could have just as well saved our money and got
> violent as hell. If you wanted to stop the line, that's the way to
> stop it. (Bruce Paulson, quoted in Casper and Wellstone, 1981:46)

The disillusionment reflected in farmer Bruce Paulson's view of
the failed attempt by rural Minnesotans to prevent the construction of a high-energy power line across their farmlands is
a sentiment increasingly shared by many Americans. Demonstrations and mass protests have become common features of
disputes over the construction of nuclear power plants, the siting of disposal sites for hazardous wastes, and the chemical
contamination of the environment. Such direct public action remains a means of inserting public input into technical decision
making, a process unusually hostile to public involvement. Often
issues with technical components have been defined as solely
technical decisions by government officials or technical experts.
The public has typically been excluded from participation both
as a result of elitist values and the barriers posed by specialized
scientific knowledge and technical jargon. When opportunities
for citizen participation have been provided, the normal mech-

anism for this input has been the public hearing. Unfortunately, such hearings generally occur too late in the decision making process, are often inconvenient and inhibiting in format, and frequently pit citizens against paid expert witnesses.

To be effective, citizen participation in scientific and technological matters must have certain characteristics. The public must be able to enter the decision-making process at an early stage. Furthermore, meaningful citizen participation requires that all segments of the public have the opportunity to take part in the policy formulation process. Outreach efforts may be necessary to ensure participation by the poor and minorities. Frequently, technical assistance will be necessary to translate existing scientific knowledge for citizens and to collect and analyze new data. Finally, if the public is to have an effective voice, ongoing means of facilitating participation will be needed. Decision making is rarely so leisurely as to permit the public the time to create a new participatory structure for each issue that must be confronted. Participatory mechanisms that provide the public with real opportunities to affect the policy process must be institutionalized.

A most innovative attempt to create such a participatory mechanism grew out of a short-lived program at the National Science Foundation (NSF). The Science for Citizens program at the NSF was established in 1977 as a result of a congressional mandate resulting from the public interest science movement (Hollander and Stoloff, 1982). The program was terminated by 1982, a victim of budget cutting by the Reagan administration. In 1978 the Science for Citizens program funded seventeen planning grants to a potpourri of organizations, ranging from a museum and a local Young Men's Christian Association (YMCA) to several universities and a medical center. Each of these groups of organizations was to use the planning funds to develop a prototype structure and organization for a public service science center in its own community or region. Then, at the end of the planning period, it could return to the NSF with a proposal for establishing and operating its center. These public service science centers were designed to provide information and technical assistance to citizens who wished to participate more effectively in community decision making. An additional goal of these centers was to increase the knowledge-able participation of both scientists and citizens in the resolution of science-related public policy matters.

In 1980, three-year operational grants were awarded for the establishment of public service centers to be located in Boston, New York, Seattle, central Appalachia, upper New England, and southwestern Michigan. This paper explores the development and first two years of operation of one of these six centers, the Science for Citizens Center of Southwestern Michigan. An examination of the structure of the center, the process by which decisions are made, and the range of activities undertaken provides insights on how citizens may be linked to technical policy making. Longitudinal data from the policy-making body of the center also provide a rare opportunity to view the internal dynamics of a participatory mechanism. The conclusion of the chapter evaluates the promise of the public service science center model for increasing the effectiveness of citizen input into matters of science and technology policy.

ESTABLISHMENT OF THE MICHIGAN CENTER

A successful application to the NSF's Science for Citizens program by the Institute of Public Affairs at Western Michigan University provided funds for the planning of the Science for Citizens Center of Southwestern Michigan (Petersen and Kaufman, 1981). The bulk of the planning for the center was carried out by a Citizens Policy Council which was composed of residents from a fifteen-county region in southwest Michigan (essentially from Grand Rapids to the Indiana border). By the end of the 8 1/2-month planning process, the council consisted of twenty-two persons and had met eleven times to devise the center's basic structure, establish some of its objectives, and develop a set of organizational bylaws.

Council meetings typically included a brief social hour and a dinner, both of which provided an opportunity for the members to interact with one another and for the group to form a sense of identity and cohesion. This was followed by the business portion of the meetings which typically consisted of presentations by staff from the center or consultants. Without exception, there was considerable discussion among the members of the council, in particular toward such questions as: How can we identify community needs? How can we reach people who need assistance? Who will provide the needed services? What kinds of services should we provide? How will we handle controversy? What kind of structure should the center have?

As might be expected, there were sharp differences over approaches and little consensus with respect to goals. Much time, for example, was taken up with discussions of the appropriate scope of a public service science center. Some council members wanted the center to concentrate on issues with a clear relation to the physical or biological sciences. Others, especially the minority members, favored a center that would also attack such problems as discrimination, unemployment, housing, and transportation. These differences led to some bitter debates, occasionally laced with charges of racism. Eventually it was decided that all proposals would be considered on a case-by-case basis and some creative compromises emerged. For example, the center initiated a science program for minority elementary students. Held in three cities, the program provides "hands-on" science experience and contact with minority scientists who can serve as role models for students. The center views the program as a means of attracting more minorities to services in science.

Another controversy developed over whether the center would function as a proactive or as a reactive agency—that is, would its services be based solely on specific requests for assistance, or would it initiate some activities on its own? In this case the council decided to emphasize reactive services. At the same time, it recognized that proactive programs might occasionally be necessary as when the council perceives a critical problem that has yet to spark public attention.

Similarly, members disagreed sharply on whether the center should engage in advocacy for citizens or simply provide information to those who request it. This issue engendered a good deal of debate but was never fully resolved. The nature of the relationship between the center and its clients continues to be worked out as programs develop.

During the planning phase, a procedure was adopted which

gave the council three separate opportunities to discuss proposals before a vote was taken. The first is an open discussion of salient issues and/or strategies. Based on that input, the staff formulates a proposal to be presented at the next meeting. At the second reading, the proposal is discussed and invariably amended, though without a formal vote. The staff then attempts to incorporate into a final draft the ideas and specific suggestions which emanate from the council. This document is presented to the members of the council as a third reading and a vote is taken. By this point in the process, most final drafts are adopted with few amendments. Using this procedure the planning process was completed with the approval of a twenty-page Final Planning Document, which contained a structure, a set of policy statements, and bylaws to govern the operations of the center.

Structure and Composition of the Center

The structure of the Science for Citizens Center consists of five main units: the Citizens Policy Council, the center staff, the Citizens Network, the Science and Professional Advisory Panel, an the Ethics and Human Values Advisory Committee. Each provides its own input to the center's operation. The Citizens Policy Council is the cornerstone of the structure, for it provides leadership through identifying goals and establishing policy. It elects its own members and officers and can amend the center bylaws. In addition, it approves all budgets including the individual budgets for all supported activities.

During the first year that the center was in operation, the Citizens Policy Council was comprised of thirty-one members: the Director and two residents from each of fifteen counties in the geographic area. The members, all volunteers, were drawn from a broad array of interest groups including the poor, senior citizens, minorities, educational institutions, governmental units, environmental groups, civic groups, agriculture, business, and industry. They ranged broadly across the age distribution with most between thirty and fifty-nine years old. While a majority were male and white, women, blacks, Hispanics, and native Americans were also well represented. On the average, their

educational levels were relatively high compared to those of
the region; they also tended to hold higher-status occupations.
Yet, their annual incomes still ranged from below $10,000 to
nearly $50,000. Such diversity, of course, is desirable, since it
ensures that a wider range of proposals will come to the attention of the center.

The center has operated with a very small staff composed of
the director, a half-time assistant director, a half-time secretary,
and several graduate and undergraduate student assistants. In
addition to coordinating activities and maintaining communication among the various components of the center, the primary
function of the staff is to receive and screen inquiries and proposals brought to the center by citizens of the region. Many of
the inquiries simply require available information or referral to
another organization and are handled by one of the staff members.

When inquiries raise more complex issues or when new research would have to be conducted in order to answer the
questions being posed, the staff will typically prepare a brief
statement for the consideration of the council. In those instances where there is substantial interest in the problem, the
council may pay a scientist or professional to develop a project
proposal in cooperation with those who brought the problem
to the center. When this is completed, the proposed project is
then considered by the council for funding.

The Citizens Network was created to augment the policy-
making role of the council, to ensure its sensitivity to the full
range of citizen needs, and to provide a necessary recruitment
device for future council members. The network is composed
of almost 200 citizens and public officials from throughout the
region. These individuals receive the center's newsletter and
provide a means of publicizing the activities of the center within
their own communities. At the same time, members of the network provide grass-roots input to the council. Often, it is a
member of the Citizens Network who first brings a local problem or controversy to the center.

Over seventy-five scientists and professionals from the region serve on the Science and Professional Advisory Panel. These
volunteers serve as an interdisciplinary roster of experts who

can be consulted on problems related to their specialties. Members of this panel sometimes informally respond to citizen inquiries. With the larger center-funded projects, members of the group frequently serve as project directors. A subset of this panel, the Consulting Associates, meets with the director of the center on a quarterly basis to provide advice on current projects, to explore means of increasing the involvement of scientists in socially relevant activities, and to identify trends in the region that may demand center attention in the future.

The final unit in the center, the Ethics and Human Values Advisory Committee, was established in response to a shift in funding at the National Science Foundation. When the NSF's Science for Citizens program was terminated before the commitment to the NSF-funded public services science centers had been fulfilled, a final year of funding was provided by the Ethics and Values in Science and Technology program at the NSF. The committee has attempted to sensitize staff, policy council members, and others involved with the center to major value issues that are related to the problems under consideration. As part of this process, the committee regularly reviews proposals and projects before the center.

The Science for Citizens Center of Southwestern Michigan has dealt with a very broad range of problems. At the end of the first full year of operations, the center had made decisions resulting in the support of a total of twelve separate projects. For ten of them, funds were provided, either for design or implementation. Of the other two, one (no. 5) was deleted due to a lack of local support, and the other (no. 6) has been held in abeyance pending resolution of political matters at the state level. A listing and brief description of all twelve projects follows:

1. Sand Dune Mining—review, analysis, and monitoring of environmental impact statements and subsequent actions dealing with sand dune mining in Michigan.

2. Career-Oriented Science Program for Minorities—being in grade school, aimed at preparation for science training in higher education.

3. Ottawa County Landfill—prepare a report on water contamination stemming from a nearby landfill.

4. Open Space/Urban Development Relationships—prepare a review and report on relationships between open space and urban development in medium-sized cities.

5. Comprehensive Plan Update, city of Bangor—deleted.

6. Public Education Program on Solid Waste for Fifteen Southwestern Michigan Counties—held in abeyance.

7. Austin Lake Reclamation Education—public education programs related to lake reclamation procedures and issues for selected audiences in a lake-shore residential area.

8. Eastern Lake Michigan Citizens Group Conference on Coastal Issues—plan and hold a general conference on issues relevant to Lake Michigan coastal areas, and develop cooperative education activities.

9. Citizen Participation Conference—plan and hold a conference to inform and alert citizens about citizen participation and its effects.

10. Eastern Equine Encephalomyelitis as a Public Health Problem—review information on the disease, its treatment, and prevention; publicize findings in a community experiencing an outbreak.

11. Black Science Night at WMU—subsidize activities of the Alliance of Minority Science Students regarding "Science Night," an event recognizing minority participation in science.

12. Analysis of Agricultural Chemicals Related to Certification Standards for Organically Grown Foods in Michigan—Review research related to characteristics of chemicals used in "organic" agriculture and prepare report suitable for presentation to farmers.

Since the first year of operation of the center, the policy council has considered about forty additional project proposals These included such topics as the future of the Kalamazoo River, preventive nutrition for the Hispanic community, the status of women in science, health education for migrant workers, nuclear war prevention, strip mining in Michigan, and groundwater contamination. Nearly twenty-five of the proposals were funded by the center. In other cases, a search for outside funding was authorized or, in a few cases, the proposals were simply rejected. Center funding of projects has normally been modest with the funds assigned to a single project rarely exceeding $5,000.

Policy Council Views

As the major decision-making unit in the center, the Citizens Policy Council and the views of its members are of central interest to observers of public interest science. During the initial planning period and during each year of operation, members of the policy council were surveyed about council proceedings, issues facing the region, and satisfaction with center development. At four points—the midpoint and end of the planning phase, the end of the first year, and the end of the second year— the members were asked to identify the most significant problems facing southwestern Michigan. As part of a check on the representativeness of the policy council, questionnaires used at the midpoint of the planning process were also sent to the pool of individuals who had been nominated for membership on the council but had not been selected.[2]

Identification of Issues

Table 3.1 contains the results of an open-ended question asking both council members and the pool of council nominees to indicate the most significant problems in southwestern Michigan with which the Science for Citizens Center ought to be concerned. Although there are some differences in frequency of response and relative rankings of topics, the overall conclusion is that the two sets are quite similar. In both cases, energy is mentioned most frequently, with land use and water quality not far behind. In addition, the two groups both ranked pollution and waste disposal among the top half-dozen topics.

Similarly, another item provided a list of six topics and asked the respondents to indicate whether he or she perceived them as very important, somewhat important, or not important. The responses were then weighted to produce summary scores, which in turn resulted in a rank ordering of the topics. For both sets of respondents, this procedure resulted in the *same* rank order of topics: (1) energy, (2) air and water quality, (3) transportation, (4) community development, (5) substance abuse, and (6) family planning. These findings, therefore, clearly indicate a rather remarkable degree of consistency between the

Table 3.1
Distribution of the Most Significant Problems in Southwestern Michigan—Council and Pool of Nominees

Problem	Rank	Frequency Within Council		Rank	Frequency Within Pool	
Energy	1	9	19.1%	1	12	26.7%
Environment	2	6	12.8		–	–
Land Use	3.5	5	10.6	2	8	17.9
Water Quality	3.5	5	10.6	3.5	7	15.6
Pollution	5.5	4	8.5	5	5	11.1
Waste Disposal	5.5	4	8.5	3.5	7	15.6
Conservation	7.5	3	6.4	8	1	2.2
Unemployment	7.5	3	6.4			–
Transportation	10	2	4.3	6	3	6.7
Education	10	2	4.3			–
Health	10	2	4.3	7	2	4.4
Housing	12.5	1	2.1			–
Discrimination	12.5	1	2.1			–

—Indicates no usable response in the category.

members of the planning stage policy council and the larger pool of individuals from which they were drawn.

In the questionnaires distributed at the end of the planning phase and at the end of each of the first two years of operation, the policy council members were again asked to rank a set of specific problems in order of their importance to southwestern Michigan. The results of these efforts are presented in Table

Table 3.2
Comparison of Rank Orderings of Problems: Final Planning Stage,
First-Year, and Second-Year Policy Councils

Problem	Final Planning Stage Mean Rank Score	Rank Order	First Year Mean Rank Score	Rank Order	Second Year Mean Rank Score	Rank Order
Energy	5.2	1	5.3	1	8.3	10
Waste Disposal	5.4	2	6.0	3	5.7	3
Land Use	5.8	3	7.3	8	6.3	6
Water Quality	6.2	4	5.9	2	6.4	7.5
Unemployment	6.9	5	8.9	12	5.8	4
Environment	7.4	6.5	6.1	4	5.2	1
Education	7.4	6.5	6.4	5	5.3	2
Pollution	7.9	8	6.5	6	6.2	5
Conservation of Resources	8.0	9	6.7	7	6.6	9
Nuclear Safety	8.9	10	9.3	13	9.4	14
Health	9.0	11	7.8	9	6.4	7.5
Air Quality	9.6	12.5	8.6	11	8.9	12
Housing	9.6	12.5	9.4	14	9.5	15
Transportation	10.0	14	10.0	15	9.3	13
Discrimination	10.5	15	8.1	10	8.7	11

3.2. Looking first at the final planning stage, energy matters
were again perceived as the most important problem facing
southwestern Michigan, followed by waste disposal, land use,
and water quality. Problems that were perceived by this group
as less important to the region included discrimination, transportation, housing, and air quality.

The survey of first-year council members bears out these and
the earlier findings in large measure. Energy was still ranked
at the very top, with waste disposal and water quality close
behind. Similarly, transportation, housing, and air quality continued to be perceived as less important. Land use declined
rather sharply in importance as compared to its rank at the end
of the planning period. Discrimination, in contrast, increased
in its perceived priority. It had been the lowest-ranked problem
during the planning period, but the first-year policy council
ranked it tenth of fifteen problems.

When we compare the responses of second-year council
members with the earlier evaluations, there are some clear sim-
ilarities and some striking differences as well. Housing, nuclear
safety, air quality, and transportation all continued to be ranked
quite low. Similarly, waste disposal continued to remain among
the top three. It is surprising to note, however, that energy
(which had been the top-ranked problem in each of the earlier
evaluations) was ranked tenth by the second-year council
members. Perhaps this is a reflection of the decreased salience
of energy problems during a period of relatively abundant petroleum supplies. During the second year of center operation,
environment and education moved to the top two positions.

When all four sets of rankings are placed together and average rank scores are calculated (see Table 3.3), an overall pattern
begins to emerge.[3] First, looking at the top six issues listed,
there is remarkable overall consistency. In only four cases is
there even one issue ranked out of the top six (land use among
first-year council members; pollution among final planning stage;
water quality and, of course, energy, among second-year council members). Similarly, of the bottom six issues listed, four
were consistently ranked among the least important by all four
groups of respondents. Add transportation to those, and the
bottom is completed.

To summarize, the average scores found in the last column of Table 3.3, then, would seem to represent a measure of consensus across the span of time represented by the four separate surveys. Energy and the environment are of primary importance, followed by the disposal of wastes, water quality, and land use. At the other end of the spectrum, housing and transportation are perceived as relatively unimportant, along with discrimination, air quality, and nuclear safety. The differences that do appear in the table are generally of small magnitude, probably representing changes in council membership or contextual effects at the time of the evaluations.

Council Satisfaction

In addition to providing information relative to the identification of salient issues, the evaluation process provided comparisons of the degree to which the members were satisfied with the procedures and activities of the policy council and of the center itself. At the end of the planning stage, at the end of the first year, and again at the end of the second year, each member was asked to respond to a set of nine items, all requiring either a positive or negative response (i.e., satisfaction or dissatisfaction). The results are presented in Table 3.4.

Beginning with an overview, it is immediately clear that the members of the policy council have been quite pleased with the procedures and activites of the policy council and the center staff. In every case, a strong majority reported satisfaction. In fact, only three items the chair's handling of meetings and statements by consultants, among first-year members, and the council's relationship with the public, among all three groups of members received positive responses from less than three-quarters of the members responding. We also asked each member to provide us with an overall rating of satisfaction on a scale from 1 to 10. At the end of the planning stage, the average was 8.3, indicating that they were obviously satisfied. The average for the same item at the end of the first year was 7.1, indicating a clear decline, but by the end of the second year it had climbed to 7.8, almost back to its initial level.

A brief comparison of the results from the first-year members

Table 3.3

Comparison of Rankings: Midpoint Planning, Final Planning, First-Year, and Second-Year Policy Councils

Problem	Mid-Point Planning	Final Planning	First Year	Second Year	Average
Energy	1	1	1	10	1
Environment	2	6.5	4	1	2
Land Use	3.5	3	8	6	5
Water Quality	3.5	4	3	3	3
Waste Disposal	5.5	2	3	3	3
Pollution	5.5	8	6	5	7
Conservation	7.5	9	7	9	9
Unemployment	7.5	5	12	4	8
Transportation	10	14	15	13	14
Education	10	6.5	5	2	6
Health	10	11	9	7.5	10
Housing	12.5	12.5	14	15	15
Discrimination	12.5	15	10	11	13
Air Quality	-	12.5	11	12	11
Nuclear Safety	-	10	13	14	12

—Indicates no usable response in the category.

Table 3.4
**Comparison of Satisfaction with Policy Council Procedures
and Activities**

		Final Planning Stage	Percent Satisfied First Year	Change	Second Year	Change
a.	The manner in which Policy Council meetings were handled by the chair.	93.3	70.0	-23.3	85.0	+15.0
b.	The orderliness by which discussion and votes were handled within the Council.	86.7	75.0	-11.7	85.0	+10.0
c.	The manner in which the Center staff served the Council.	100.0	90.0	-11.7	92.0	+ 2.0
d.	The working relationships among the Policy Council members.	100.0	93.8	- 6.2	91.0	- 2.8
e.	The Council's record-keeping, especially the extent to which it enabled members to keep track of what had been decided at past meetings.	100.0	85.0	-15.0	92.0	+ 7.0
f.	The Policy Council's recommendations.	93.3	83.3	-10.0	92.0	+ 8.7
g.	The Policy statements provided by consultants.	80.0	70.6	- 9.4	85.0	+14.4
h.	The contributions of the other members of the Policy Council.	100.0	100.0	0.0	100.0	0.0
i.	The Policy Council's relationship with the public.	63.6	52.9	-10.7	62.0	+ 9.1

with the results from the other two surveys, however, raises an interesting question. In every case with the exception of the contributions of other members, which was stable, the members were *less* satisfied at the end of the first year of center operations than the members were at the end of the planning stage. Furthermore, in at least one instance (the handling of meetings by the chair of the council), the amount of decline was substantial (23.3%). While it could be reflecting the changing composition of the council (given the relatively small numbers involved), this pattern of change *might* indicate an absolute decline in the policy council's general level of satisfaction.

A look at the results of the second year, however, reveals that in every case but one (working relationships among council members), the level of satisfaction increased over the levels reported at the end of the first year. In most cases, they constituted a "recovery" to the levels reported at the end of the planning stage (one—the statements provided by consultants— reached its high point of 85.0%). Whatever the reason for the apparent decline at the end of the first year, it did not appear to affect the members at the end of the second year of operations.

Some clues as to the changes in the levels of satisfaction come from a section of the evaluation instruments dealing with problems. Here, the three sets of council members were asked to respond to a battery of potential problems, indicating the frequency with which they were perceived to occur (i.e., often, sometimes, never). Table 3.5 contains those results.

Looking first at the final planning stage survey, it is clear that a majority was aware of a number of problems with the center. The council members identified all but three of the areas listed as being problematic either sometimes or often. Only unorganized meetings, domination by the project director/staff, and lack of representation were perceived by these members as *not* being problems. After a year of operation, the reports of the council members indicate that the situation had not improved significantly. Indeed, one of the three areas that had previously been singled out as a success (i.e., representation) came to be perceived as a problem. By the end of the second year, though, the situation had changed substantially. Fully six

Table 3.5
Comparison of Perceived Problems

Item		Percent Viewing Item as a Problem Sometimes or Often				
		Final Planning Stage	First Year	Change	Second Year	Change
a.	Uninvolved members	53.3	68.8	+15.5	70.0	+ 1.2
b.	Membership unrepresentative of the Council's clientele.	33.3	56.3	+23.0	30.0	-26.3
c.	Lack of attendence	80.0	87.5	+ 7.5	69.0	-18.5
d.	Lack of information	60.0	68.8	+ 8.8	46.0	-22.8
e.	Domination by a few members.	92.3	83.3	- 9.0	85.0	+ 1.7
f.	No clear goals.	80.0	52.9	-27.1	46.0	- 6.9
g.	No clear priorities.	86.7	64.7	-22.0	46.0	-18.7
h.	Domination by Project Director/staff.	14.3	23.5	+ 9.2	33.0	+ 9.5
i.	Unorganized meetings.	14.3	22.2	+ 7.9	46.0	+23.8
j.	Lack of publicity.	50.0	64.7	+14.7	85.0	+20.3
k.	Too much time on unimportant issues.	80.0	88.9	+ 8.9	84.0	- 4.9

of the eleven items were perceived as problematic by less than a majority, and in several cases the change represented a substantial turnaround (e.g., representation, lack of information, lack of priorities). With only two of the items (lack of organization and publicity) was there any appreciable increase in concern.

The previous findings with respect to satisfaction should be kept in mind, however. Since they clearly indicate a substantial degree of satisfaction, the problems being reported must not be particularly serious or long-lasting in character. Still, they help explain the apparent decline and recovery in levels of satisfaction. This is especially clear when one looks at the columns in the table which contain the amounts of change across surveys. Of the eleven areas listed, eight were perceived as problematic by more of the council members at the end of the first year than by the council members at the end of the planning stage. Similarly, at the end of the second year, four of those same areas were perceived as problematic by fewer of the members. Moreover, coupling with this fact that representation had earlier been viewed as one of the center's strong points, it is not surprising that the council members' level of satisfaction first declined and then recovered.

Client Satisfaction

While the perceptions of members of the Citizens Policy Council provide valuable insights into the strengths and limitations of the center, an even more direct measure of success is provided by the reaction of citizens who requested assistance from the center. During the first few months of the center's existence, considerable time was spent in developing a mass media campaign and in designing procedures for handling inquiries and requests by citizens. Even as this preliminary work was being done, however, requests for assistance began to trickle into the center. By the end of January 1981, requests had been logged in on twenty-nine occasions. The number exceeded 100 by February 1982.

A brief interview schedule was designed for use in telephone interviews with those who had contacted the center. The schedule concentrated on how the person had learned of the center, the services performed by center staff, the respondent's level of satisfaction with his or her contact with the center, and the quality of any subsequent contacts with the center. A random sample of fifty cases was drawn to keep costs down. Due to duplication and other problems (e.g., moved, disconnected, wrong number), thirty-five persons were available for interview. Of this group, twenty-six (75%) were interviewed by telephone. This amounts to a 26 percent sample of the total population of clients.

It was discovered that only five persons had learned of the Science for Citizens Center through mass media coverage. The most common ways in which citizens had learned of the center were through mailings from the center, personal contact with the center director, and by referral from Western Michigan University departments or offices. During the interviews many respondents expressed a desire for more information about the center and its programs.

Clients also reported receiving a variety of services from the center and its staff. Eleven people received information on scientific topics. Four others received names of references and/or contacts for further information. Two people asked for and received critiques of proposals. Four people requested a member of the center as a speaker at a public meeting. Only four persons received no services from the center. This was a result of the center not being capable of providing the expected services. Finally, one person expressed dissatisfaction with the fact that the center would not play a strong advocacy role.

Those interviewed, by and large, were quite satisfied with the services they received from center staff. Six respondents (23%) reported that they were "very satisfied" with the services they had received, while seventeen citizens (65%) indicated that they were "satisfied." Only three people (12%) expressed dissatisfaction. In all cases the respondents felt the center had not gone far enough in providing the services they had expected.

Of the twenty-six interviewed, sixteen (62%) had no subsequent interaction with the center after their initial contact with the staff. Ten persons (38%), however, indicated that they had developed further contacts. Only one of these persons who reported contacts beyond an initial one indicated any dissatisfaction with these contacts. During its start-up period the center staff was able to respond to the relatively light flow of inquiries and requests in a manner which satisfied 90 percent of those interviewed. Some confusion about center goals and services did exist among respondents and many expressed a desire for more information about the center.

The Center in Operation

The Science of Citizens Center of Southwestern Michigan is a broad-spectrum public service science center. No possible project is ruled out on the basis of subject matter alone. Not all the NSF-funded science centers have taken this approach. Some, such as the Consumer Health Policy Information and Resource Center in New York City, are more narrowly focused.

One consequence of a broad scope of concern is that a great deal of time is spent in allocating resources. When citizens bring very simple requests to the center, the staff may be able to promptly meet their needs. When more extensive services are required, however, an elaborate screening process is set into motion. The staff works with citizens to develop a brief proposal to go before the Citizens Policy Council. This body then debates the significance of the problem and may vote a small budget for the development of a full-scale proposal. Then a project director is hired to serve as a consultant to the citizens in the preparation of a fully developed proposal. This then goes before the council for further debate. While this process helps ensure that proposals are thoughtfully developed, it creates problems in responding to community needs in a timely fashion. The speed-of-response problem is also aggravated by the heavy dependence on volunteers and part-time personnel who have many other commitments.

The slowness with which some projects developed has been a source of concern to the policy council and solving this problem may require that the center narrow its scope of concern. The basis for such a narrowing may be emerging. The first dozen projects funded by the center stressed, with only a few exceptions, environmental issues and science education. The questionnaire data presented earlier also reveals that when policy council members were asked to identify the most significant issues facing southwestern Michigan, the highest-ranking responses were energy and such environmental issues as land use, water quality, and waste disposal. It is also true, however, that the priority attached to some issues such as education and unemployment rose over the period of the council's existence. Whether this was due to the changing composition of the council or changes in attitude resulting from council debate remains unclear.

At the end of the planning period one council member lamented that the council's decision making had become so political. Yet, how could it be otherwise? The council had no device for limiting the scope of the center and no procedures for setting general priorities. Everything was handled on a case-by-case basis. After all, the allocation of resources is the very stuff of politics.

In the model developed by the Science for Citizens Center of Southwestern Michigan, a great deal of the responsibility for the success of the center is located in the staff. Unfortunately, the scope of center activities often overloads the small staff. It must be prepared to provide prompt responses and referrals to citizen inquiries on an unlimited range of topics. Furthermore, they play a critical role in translating and shaping public concerns into specific projects which may obtain funding through policy council attention. In doing so, they inevitably serve as a filter between the policy council and the public. This may be essential in order for the council to operate as a governing board with broad oversight authority. At times, however, the council has felt isolated from the action and has demanded that the staff provide more detailed information on the status of projects.

The evaluation of client satisfaction revealed that the overwhelming majority of initial users of the center were satisfied with the services they received from the staff. As the volume of client demand increases, however, maintaining satisfaction may become more difficult. Heavier dependence on the Professional Advisory Panel through referrals is a possible solution. This, though, poses other problems. The reward structure of universities provides little support for the small-scale applied activity that citizen inquiries generally require. It may be difficult to maintain the commitment of scientist volunteers over a sustained period of time.

THE FUTURE OF PUBLIC SERVICE SCIENCE CENTERS

Despite having been traditionally excluded from decision making on scientific and technical issues, citizens have a right to participate in such matters. This right can be justified on a variety of grounds. In a democracy citizens have a right to participate in decisions with major social consequences. Many scientific and technological developments pose very real risks to society and those who are placed at risk have a moral right to participation. Furthermore, public involvement may be necessary to gain legitimacy for controversial decisions and may contribute to the practice of science (Carroll, 1971; Holman and Dutton, 1978).

If citizens are to participate effectively in decisions with a substantial scientific content, they are going to require technical assistance. As Nelkin and Pollak (1979:62) observe, many social disputes are translated into technical terms and any resolution requires a reasonable distribution of the critical political resource of expertise. The recent controversy in Minnesota over the construction of high-energy power lines illustrates the consequences of a maldistribution of this resource. Casper and Wellstone's (1981) eloquent account of the fight by Minnesota farmers to prevent the construction of this line points out that intense feelings, protests, and even the use of violence were inadequate in stopping the line. The farmers lacked the technical experts who could effectively challenge the authorities from the power cooperatives that were constructing the line. The cooperatives were able to limit the scope of the dispute to a set of technical issues and easily beat the farmers in a series of public hearings and judicial proceedings.

Community-based public service science centers such as the six funded by the National Science Foundation look like a most promising means of providing technical assistance to citizens. Such ongoing community institutions can provide technical assistance to citizens on a wide range of topics, permitting earlier and more informed participation by citizens in the decision-making process than normally occurs. Local centers also permit a more personal and individualized approach than would be feasible with many alternatives. The necessity of such responsive adaptation to local needs was stressed by Robbins (1977) who, in assessing technology transfer programs, found that the most successful programs recognized that mere access to information is not enough, that information must be translated into useful forms, that face-to-face interaction is essential, and that solutions must be adapted to local problems.

No comprehensive evaluation of the six NSF-funded centers has been conducted. Available information does reveal, however, that these centers have facilitated informed and effective participation by citizens in the resolution of a number of community issues. The evaluations of the Science for Citizens Center of Southwestern Michigan reveal a high degree of satisfaction with the performance of the center by both members of the Citizens Policy Council and by citizens who made inquiries and requests to the center.

On the other hand, some difficulties experienced by the centers are apparent. Much like the environmental movement in general, the centers have been dominated by the middle class. Most have reported problems with outreach efforts designed to increase the involvement of the poor and minorities. Furthermore, one of the results of NSF sponsorship was that the NSF's tradition of political neutrality often inhibited local centers. They were unable to develop a clear position with respect to relationships with the political structure. As a result, the centers were not as politically effective as they might have been.

Still, on balance, the public service centers have accomplished a good deal with very modest budgets. Public service science is unquestionably needed in our society. Its short-term future seems in doubt, however. The elimination of funding for the Science for Citizens program from the 1982 NSF budget cut short an experiment in the redistribution of expertise. A third year of NSF funding was provided by another foundation program, but the centers have now exhausted this federal funding. The center in Boston has effectively gone out of business, being folded into an existing community organization. The future of the other centers seems uncertain. Individual memberships or local foundations may be possible sources of funds. In better economic times local government bodies might have been likely funding sources. At present, however, municipalities throughout the country are having trouble providing such basic services as police and fire protection and can ill afford to fund new ventures.

Much of the voluntary sector is currently looking to the corporate world for support, but this poses special problems for public service science centers. Since industrial firms are frequently targets of environmental groups and concerned citizens, it seems unlikely that corporations will fund bodies that will serve as sources of support to their antagonists. Power is not generally given up that easily. And in any case public service science centers which took corporate funds might jeopardize their independence. Certainly the legitimacy of the centers to the public would be compromised.

Perhaps the most that can be hoped for at present are small-scale efforts largely staffed by volunteers. Such centers could develop a firm groundwork for more extensive programs in the future when the government might be more receptive to real citizen participation. The issue facing Americans will increasingly contain scientific and technical components. If citizens are actively to shape their futures, they must establish the participatory mechanisms that will link the public with the decision-making processes of science and technology.

NOTES

1. Professor Petersen's work was supported in part by a fellowship and grant from the Faculty Research Fund, Western Michigan University.

2. Procedures and instruments varied to some degree, across the several evaluations, as did response rates. For example, the response rate for the midpoint survey of Planning Stage Policy Council members was 100 percent, in contrast to 68 percent for the survey of the council at the end of the planning stage, 77 percent of the first-year council members, and 79 percent of the members in the second year. While such variations do undoubtedly allow for the possibility of error, we feel that the substantial degree of consistency provides a sufficient foundation for the comparability of results.

3. Since the midpoint instrument contained only thirteen response categories and the others contained fifteen, standardization was called

for. Therefore, the individual rankings for each instrument were calculated as percentages of the sum of the total ranks possible for that instrument. These percentages were then simply averaged across the several evaluations.

REFERENCES

Carroll, James D. 1971
    "Participatory Technology," *Science* 171:647–53.
Casper, Barry M., and Paul D. Wellstone 1981
    Powerline. (Amherst: University of Massachusetts Press).
Hollander, Robert D., and James Stoloff 1982
    "Institutionalizing Public Service Science: Its Perils and Promise," *Journal of Voluntary Action Research* 11:34–45.
Holman, Henry R., and Dennis B. Dutton 1978
    "A Case for Public Participation in Science Policy Formation and Practice," *Southern California Law Review* 51:1505–34.
Nelkin, Dorothy, and Michael Pollak 1979
    "Public Participation in Technological Decisions" *Technology Review* 81:8, 55–64.
Petersen, James C., and Robert W. Kaufman 1981
    "Public Service Science Centers," *Citizen Participation* 2:20–23.
Robbins, Michael D. 1977
    "Factors Leading to the Success and Failure of Complex Technology Transfer Programs." Report prepared for the Energy Research and Development Administration. Washington, D.C.: Government Printing Office.

4

Beyond Technocracy: Anticipatory Democracy in Government and the Marketplace

CLEMENT BEZOLD

Each of us spend much more time interacting with the marketplace and the products it makes available than we spend interacting with government and its products. Citizens around the country are trying to take a more conscious part in steering the future course of their communities. This chapter, growing out of those public attempts at "anticipatory democracy," will explore the ways in which consumers can influence the products which research and development (R&D) seek to place on the market. In effect, consumers vote with their dollars, but those votes come after the choices are defined. We will move beyond technocracy (bureaucratic and technologically driven decision making) in the marketplace as in government, when the public becomes actively involved in influencing the development of the choices offered by government and the market.

This is a critical need, in part because of the nature of technological innovation. As David Collingridge has pointed out:

Our technological competence vastly exceeds our understanding of the social effects which follow from its exercise. This poses the dilemma of control: when change is easy, the need for it cannot be foreseen; when the need for change is apparent, change has become expensive, difficult and time consuming. (1980:11)

Collingridge argues that the impact on society of many technologies cannot be anticipated. Therefore, mechanisms are needed to adjust the technology after its ill effects have been identified. While some controls are needed after products are put on the market, there are more important opportunities for consumers consciously to shape the future products they would like to buy. This would happen by enabling consumers to identify the types of social conditions they prefer and to relate those societal preferences to the possibilities which research and development efforts could provide.

CITIZEN PARTICIPATION

One interpretation of the history of citizen participation in policy issues is that it has shown an evolution of techniques in which citizens first simply complained about policies and programs after they were implemented, then learned to react to nearly completed proposals, then demanded to take part in designing policies and programs, and finally became involved in designing sets of policies into alternative visions for the future of their communities (Bezold, 1977; Bezold, 1978a; Rosenbaum, 1978). While the last stages of this evolution have only begun to take place, and citizens and students of policy making need to keep this evolution in view, a similar evolution is necessary in the marketplace, particularly in the rapdily moving fields we collectively call the communications revolution and the biological revolution.

This chapter will explore the movement toward "anticipatory democracy," or more future-conscious participation in the public sector. Then moving to the private sector, this chapter will review the nature of research and development (a key to industrial innovation and new products) along with general trends in technology and in society—trends suggesting that, just as the industrial revolution required certain types of technologies and products, the "third wave," postindustrial era is already bringing new types of technologies and products with attendant opportunities and threats. Finally, the requirements for "anticipatory democracy" in the marketplace (linking citizens and consumers more consciously to the forces which generate new products) will be explored along with some mechanisms that might not meet those requirements. A critical element of the argument here is that the marketplace lacks the capacity (which the public sector has begun to develop) whereby the general public can take part in "inventing" desirable technological futures and in relating these to the types of products and services that research and development efforts could produce.

REINTEGRATING THE FUTURE IN PUBLIC DECISION MAKING

At the end of *Future Shock*, Alvin Toffler prescribed "anticipatory democracy" as the cure to rapid change and the accompanying sense of disenfranchisement (Toffler, 1970; 1978). Anticipatory democracy includes a variety of forms of more future-conscious participation in organizations, corporations, educational institutions, and governments (Bezold, 1978a). Toffler identified a variety of goals and futures programs as examples of efforts to get more genuine participation that was also more future-oriented. In 1978, David Baker (1978) identified forty-four state, local, and regional programs of this type. In 1982, the Institute for Alternative Futures added several more to the list (Bezold, Jones, Wilson, 1982).

The earliest forms of these programs were efforts such as Goals for Georgia or Goals for Dallas—efforts that primarily sought to gain public awareness of, support for, and assistance in implementing a particular set of goals. A next refinement has been what I call "goals with forecasts" programs, such as Texas 2000 or Illinois 2000. These programs usually gather and publish the forecasts that underlie current policy making. Goals are then set on the basis of these forecasts for economic and population growth, for energy use, for government revenues, and so on. The third stage are "goals with futures" programs such as Alternative for Washington and the work of the Hawaii Commission on the Year 2000. In these programs, the forecasts of the "official future" (those used in the "goals with forecasts" programs) are supplemented by a wider range of possibilities. Rather than assuming one singular future, this third group actually generates several differing sets of assumptions about what the plausible and the preferable futures for the state or community might be.

The nature and extent of public involvement varies widely in each of the three sets of programs, with the most effective involvement in programs such as Alternative for Washington (AFW). In AFW, the governor appointed to the group a representative cross section (150 persons) of the state to devise the original alternatives. These 150 people identified eleven different images for the state and then estimated how policy choices in areas such as housing, transportation, and health would relate to one or more of the futures. These images were refined at regional meetings where 1,500 additional people took part in framing the choices. The choices were then packaged into a variety of ballot forms and given in person, through the mail, through random sample polls, and through a newspaper questionnaire (accompanied by a major Sunday supplement in most of the state's major newspapers and public television programs). In all, about 60,000 people took part in this first phase. A second phase, in which costs, priorities, and trade-offs were established, involved almost 40,000 people. Other programs have not been as committed to public involvement, many of them using a typically elitist "commission" approach. While this can and has produced useful results, the capacity to share the task of exploring and shaping the community's future is diminished.

There are several lessons from these various programs. The most relevant is that those programs that are able to explore the assumptions which underlie current policy making, that are able to invent various plausible and preferable images of the future for the state or community (ideally involving as many people as possible in this invention process), and that can relate those futures to current policy choices and spending priorities (again involving as many people as possible in this choice process) will have significantly altered the nature of normal bureaucratic or technocratic politics. As DeSario noted in chapter 1, technocracy for our purposes "is the application of technical knowledge, expertise, techniques, and methods to problem solving." The goals and futures programs are one way to share technical knowledge with the public. However, these programs are not panaceas. They require significant "political capital" on the part of the top elected official (the mayor or governor) and active involvement of the planning office and of the council members or legislative leadership. They also require a commitment by business and citizen groups to take part in an involved and complex process which may or may not end up backing their original positions. In all, it requires a "high standard of advocacy" and an openness for the policy to engage in a sophisticated and ongoing discussion. Given the myriad disincentives in most communities, it is amazing that there has been as much experimentation over the last two decades as there has been.

For the typical citizen, such programs give the opportunity to take a more conscious part in exploring the major decisions the communities' officials will confront well before they arrive in the form of a crisis. Sidney Verba and Norman Nie (1972) examined the patterns of political participation in America and noted the decline in what they called "communalists" citizens who had a distinct sense of political efficacy because of their efforts on community projects. Verba and Nie hypothesized that the decline in communalists they saw was associated with the decline in small towns. Others argue that the community spirit of the small town has been growing. Hazel Henderson (1978b), for example, has argued that there has been a wider range of citizen movements in rural areas and urban areas of all sizes which reflect the attempt to improve the community. Part of the sense of alienation with electoral participation is the recognition that the choice between candidates seldom makes a meaningful difference (Bezold, 1979). In this context, futures programs make the problems and opportunities of the future more visible, given the voter and nonvoter the opportunity to speculate and dream about what they might want the community to be and to relate that image to current decisions. Thus, it is in this area, the envisioning of possibilities and their relation to current choices, that the anticipatory democracy efforts will make the greatest contribution toward overcoming the technocratically created future.

But government does not do everything; in fact, most of our lives are shaped in private or in the private sector. Technocratic decision making is an equally large problem in the marketplace.

VALUES AND BIASES OF MARKETPLACE DECISIONS

What are the major forces that steer the future of the products and services which are bought and sold in the marketplace? Where do the individual's values enter into the sequence? What are the challenges posed by science and technology applied to the marketplace in the years ahead? What are the analogs in the marketplace to the futures program in the public sector described above?

R&D: Who Decides and for What?

The United States is an advanced industrial nation. Research and development (R&D) efforts are funded in part by governments and foundations but even more so (particularly for the development of specific products) by private companies. In market systems, consumers generally are limited to saying yes or no via their purchases after a product has been developed and marketed. In this setting, as Charles Lindblom (1977) points out, consumers delegate to corporations the discretion to make all decisions instrumental to production, not only R&D but plant location, the degree of enviromental protection beyond governmentally mandated levels, the degree of automation of production, and other important decisions. In regard to innovation, Lindblom notes that

market systems operate with at least one major bias toward innovation. Buyers and sellers are ordinarily free to engage in transactions without regard to adverse effects on third parties. Hence business enterprises are free to introduce new products and new technologies without regard for the skills, enterprises, or communities they destroy in doing so. . . . Tiny minorities of one or a few can innovate, regardless of its impacts (whereas other decision-making forums allow vetoes by minorities—including the public sector where business groups often exercise the minority veto). (1977:12)

While Lindblom is raising a large array of issues, the topic here is the ways in which the public can take a more proactive part in shaping the technological innovation which will, in turn, shape society.

Recent years have seen the rise of a variety of corporate responsibility efforts, though few as yet have focused on responsibility in innovation. Alvin Toffler (1980) has argued that companies will develop multiple bottom lines beyond the single bottom line of profit. Companies take the risk of investing R&D funds on what they hope to be successful products. What criteria guide them? Joseph Coates (1977) argues that the three criteria are: Will it work? Will it sell? Is it safe? In anticipating the side effects, the externalities or social costs of a product are left out of the costs borne by the producers and consumers of that product. Robert Gee (1977), a corporate planner in the chemical industry, provides a list of "relatively simple risk-reward criterion to guide resource allocation decisions" for research programs. Is the program:

related to profits?

useful in communication between research people and business management?

explicit and quantitative so that assumptions can be examined?

as free as possible from research optimism?

adjusted to reflect uncertainty?

focused on the critical variables which will ultimately influence profitability?

derived from estimates and forecasts for which R&D is responsible?

related to the real-world marketplace and does it convey to corporate management an awareness of practical business aspects?

These criteria would be adequate if they produced no serious effects, including waste of research, production, and distribution capacities. Yet the externalities resulting from these criteria are often a serious problem. As Marshall McLuhan noted, once we shape our tools, our tools shape us. These criteria don't reflect the fact that technology plays a critical role in shaping society. As we shall see, the anticipatory projects suggest some ways that are compatible with their image of a preferred society.

A common argument that arises from the operation of criteria such as these is that of a "technological imperative" in which technology for technology's sake becomes common (Winner, 1977). One report on industrial innovation estimated that "capacity push" (what the company can do) or a "technological imperative" accounts for 40 percent of innovations (Uhlmann, 1977); another argued that market demands or needs accounted for all but 20 to 40 percent of important innovations sampled in a large number of fields (Utterback et al., 1977). Thus, R&D funds may be spent on new products that are not necessarily improvements over existing products. In the pharmaceutical R&D marketplace, there have often been financial incentives for developing marginally better drugs in order to get a share of a lucrative market. A parallel problem is the tendency of the market to emphasize high-technology items where they are profitable. These two problems are exacerbated by yet another. Whether a product reflects market needs or not, products can be sold, if given adequate promotion, regardless of their contribution to the individual's needs or social conditions (Galbraith, 1967).

The federal government in the United States has seldom confronted these questions directly. Federal support for innovation is often for innovation's sake. As Leonard Lederman (1977), a federal government official and student of the innovation process, has put it, "there are no well-defined criteria with which to formulate normative judgements about the rate and direction of innovation." Yet, just as there have been experiments in "anticipatory democracy" in the public sector, there have been important developments in the area of R&D and innovation, developments which address both the participation question and the issue of the citizen/consumer criteria for products. But before turning to these, it is relevant to ask what particular trends in society and technology might have a shaping influence on industrial innovation.

TRENDS IN SOCIETY AND TECHNOLOGY

In the area of technology, John and Magda McHale (1979) have argued that increasingly "ephemeral" technologies, which involve less resource depletion and are very energy efficient and low in environmental impact, will become common. The McHales have traced the history of technology and noted three distinct phases in industrial technologies. The first phase— roughly from 1850 to 1980—included steel, railroads, petroleum, electrical generation, and the automobile; the second phase—from 1950 to 1980—focused more on products such as light metals, plastics, electronics, and airplanes. We are at the beginning of the third phase, which, they argue, will emphasize a variety of bioconversion and biotechnical developments. Figure 4.1 shows these phases. The newer technologies of the third phase will require less of a trade-off between growth and environmental degradation or energy consumption, the McHales argue. Because the key aspect of this third phase is the emergence of information or organized knowledge as the basic resource, and this can be shared without being depleted, "the struggle for human survival will become more and more of a non-zero sum game; success or gain will be predicated more on sharing of advantage, on all winning" (1979:16). Citizen participation in government and as consumers will be an important component of that sharing of advantage.

The Third Wave

The McHales' argument coincides with Alvin Toffler's analysis of the movement of the United States and other advanced industrial nations beyond industrial civilization. In *The Third Wave*, Toffler (1980) argues that agriculture civilization was the first wave, industrial civilization the second, and that we are entering the third wave, a fundamental change into a new civilization with its own set of "axial principles" and social arrangements. The full argument is beyond the scope of this chapter. The relevance for the discussion here includes the observations that (1) the technology of the communications revolution can foster significant decentralization; (2) more diversity

Figure 4.1
Phases of Industrial Development

Early industrial practices were highly resource-intensive
and wasteful, but the third phase of industrial development,
which we are now entering, holds forth the promise of sus-
tainable growth with minimal impact.

1850	1950	1980	2000+
First Phase	Second Phase	Third Phase	
Steel Railroads Petroleum Automobile Electrical generation Etc.	Light metals Plastics Electronics Nuclear fission Computers Airlines Aerospace Etc.	Composites Industrial microbiology Enhanced bioconversion Bionics Mariculture Biochemical industries Nuclear fusion Etc.	
High visible impact due to fossil use. Great increase in materials extraction and resource depletive practices. High waste/ production ratios.		Impact decreases as new ranges of technology tend to be relatively non- resource depletive, using less energy and materials. Trend towards micro mini- aturization; more efficient regenerative practices, high waste reuse and high recycle rates.	

Source: John and Magda Cordell McHale 1979. Reprinted, with per-
mission, from *The Futurist*, published by the World Future Society,
4916 St. Elmo Ave., Bethesda, Maryland 20814.

in industrial innovation is possible because of computer-as-
sisted design and manufacturing; (3) many of the excesses that
Lindblom noted of corporations, which resulted from their focus on the monetary bottom line, will increasingly be looked
on as part of the "multiple bottom lines" which corporate ex-
ecutives must confront; (4) "prosumption," the merger of production and consumption (which the industrial revolution split),
will return as individuals do more for themselves and for their
communities.

Toffler's general argument has been confirmed by John Naisbitt's (1982) identification of ten "megatrends," based on cov-

erage of those trends in local newspapers around the United States.

There are a variety of new opportunities which technology and general trends in society are likely to present in the years ahead. Yet, as with any technology, there is the potential for undesirable side effects—for example, the use of the technologies of the communications revolution to establish a "big brother," *cum 1984*, or "disciplined" society. Simultaneously, the biological revolution will produce a variety of new products, particularly in the agricultural and health care sectors of the economy. With recombinant DNA, we have harnessed the computer programs of nature. The macromolecules such as insulin and interferon, which are too complicated for our industrial peptide chemistry operations to mimic, are produced naturally and consistently by living cells. Our knowledge of the genetic code allows us to turn cells into factories to produce what was once beyond our grasp. We will be able to adjust plants to their environment rather than the reverse, as we have with irrigation and fertilizers. Yet these same skills will also give us the ability to choose the characteristics of our offspring, giving us the capacity to shape human and other evolution more consciously than ever before.

Both the biological revolution and the communications revolution raise a host of major questions which deserve serious anticipation on the part of the public (Bezold, 1980). We need anticipatory democracy in the marketplace because many of the directions of those technological revolutions will be determined on the basis of market forces. Consumers have the option to shape proactively the future for their community. A first step is to apply more consciousness to the way in which we shape our tools (technologies), particularly as they become new products in the marketplace.

THE NEED FOR ANTICIPATORY DEMOCRACY IN THE MARKETPLACE

Two major requirements for anticipatory democracy in the marketplace are, first, an awareness of the possibilities that could result from basic and applied research, and, second, the capacity to link that awareness to value judgments and to the potential results of the research and particularly new products or service. As with the anticipatory democracy projects in the public sector, there are significant steps in the direction of these two requirements.

WORKER PLANNING

A common reaction when a factory shuts down because of lack of demand for its product has been to study what else the factory and its workers could produce. Few of these plans have ever been based on a set of criteria other than the techno-economic criteria mentioned above. Yet one of the more exciting efforts to apply a wider set of values to new product choices was undertaken by the workers in the Lucas Aerospace factories. Faced with continuing layoffs of their workforce, the shop stewards combined (the interunion body representing all of the factories) sought assistance from academics. After getting little response from that source, the shop stewards went to the workers themselves, asking what socially useful products the in-place capital and the workers at Lucas could produce. This unleashed a great deal of creativity and hundreds of ideas from the workforce of engineers and skilled craftsmen. These ideas were combined into an alternative "Corporate Plan" containing 150 potential products or product lines. The introduction to the plan noted that

the desire to work on socially useful products is one which is now widespread through large sectors of industry. The aerospace industry is a particularly glaring example of the gap which exists between that which technology could provide, and that which it actually does provide to meet the wide range of human problems we see about us. There is something seriously wrong about a society which can produce a level of technology to design a Concorde but cannot provide enough simple urban heating systems to protect old-age pensioners who are dying each year of hypothermia. (Bezold, 1978b:230)

Although the management of Lucas refused for some time to consider the plan, others in the management field recognized its importance. The British *Financial Times*, for example, called the corporate plan "one of the most radical alternative plans ever drawn up by workers for their company. . . . [It's a] twentieth-century version of the Industrial Revolution." The Lucas example has led to similar activity in several other British companies and has been discussed in the United States. Moved by a similar interest in taking part in shaping technology and preserving jobs, Glen Watts has created a Committee on the Future of his union, the Communications Workers of America.

The Lucas experience shows that new product possibilities can be related to values in a sophisticated manner. Simultaneously, the effort stimulated much discussion about the nature and definition of "socially useful" products. Michael George (who worked with the Lucas project) has identified five components to the socially useful definition.

1. At the point of production, enhancing the job control and skill/knowledge of the worker. At the point of use, avoid mystifying the consumer/user by making the user more reliant on professionalized help for maintenance and repair.

2. Pooling rather than fragmenting skill, knowledge, and expertise in production and not tending to privatise the user/consumer.

3. Tending to promote both democratic control in industrial relations (e.g., allowing proactive bargaining by workers who understand the social, economic, political, as well as production aspects) and democratic control by individuals and groups outside the work environment through social action and negotiation over the product's introduction, use, and removal.

4. Not separating the paradigm of production from that of use, not separating design and planning, and giving workers leverage of this process—both to consider product outcomes and production requirements.

5. Using less capital- and energy-intensive methods and reducing obsolescence rates. (1978:8)

This list applies the values of the Lucas workers group to production processes, products, and the economy in general. Others might apply other values for each of these. The point is that the Lucas workers have made a significant attempt to relate their values to industrial production for judging not only new products but the production processes by which they are made.

THE APPROPRIATE TECHNOLOGY MOVEMENT

Another movement, more familiar in the United States, is the appropriate technology movement. Sparked by many forces, one of which was E. F. Schumacher's work, particularly his book *Small Is Beautiful*, this movement is applying a set of values to products. In so doing, its members have, so to speak, taken the future into their own hands by evolving a consciously different image of a desirable society (Love, 1977).

Although the worker planning movement must await a favorable reaction on the part of management before its plans are implemented, the appropriate technology movement has gone directly from design to small-scale production. In fact, the movement has the equivalent of several R&D centers, places such as the Intermediate Technology Development Group in Great Britain, the Farallones Institute, the Rodale Press Research Center, the New Alchemy Institute, and the Institute for Local Self-Reliance (Ellis, 1977; Rain, 1977; Rodale, 1981).

One set of criteria for judging the products of these efforts includes the following:

sparing use of resources, preferably indigenous

strengthening decentralized, self-sufficient, relatively autonomous communities where products and consumption are integrated around basic needs provision at the local level

creation of institutions which are as close to working directly with the people as possible to insure that they will be responsive to and representative of the local community

aiding the development of small entrepreneurship and distributed capital; is employment-intensive in creating meaningful jobs. (Mackenzie, 1981:18)

There are a variety of arguments in and around the appropriate technology movement about high technology and how decentralized and self-sufficient communities should be. For example, whether space is an "appropriate technology" does not yield a simple yes or no and has led some to propose a parallel set of criteria to "advanced appropriate technology."

The point for the argument here is that the preconditions for anticipatory democracy in the marketplace—awareness of technological possibilities and the capacity to make value judgments (including judgments using nontraditional values) about those possibilities—has been demonstrated in efforts such as the worker planning and appropriate technology movements. There are a variety of other possibilities for encouraging greater future-consciousness in the marketplace.

FURTHER LINKAGES: MORE ANTICIPATORY DEMOCRACY IN THE MARKETPLACE

What are some of the ways in which the public could take a more active part in shaping the future via the marketplace? What are the steps in that process in relation to the lessons of anticipatory democracy in the public sector?

One goal analogous to that found in the futures programs is a movement toward smart and free markets rather than the dumb and unequal market conditions which often occur at present. In the marketplace, consumers are usually unequal in their capacity, vis-à-vis that of the producers, to evaluate products or to lobby the political system for their positions. At the same time the market has become "dumb" in certain areas with costly results. In automobiles, for example, the ability of the U.S. auto industry to control the market in the 1950s, 1960s, and part of the 1970s led to its decline in the 1970s and 1980s. Developing alternative scenarios for technological development would array the technological options and give a sense of the human impact of those options. Encouraging consumers to explore plausible and preferable future scenarios and to develop their own would allow consumers to clarify their values and be inventive in considering their ongoing expenditures.

Another goal is the consideration of what research and development in specific fields could bring. In other words, what are the R&D efforts that consumers would like to see; what new products (given the variety of consumer's values) would they want to buy? Consumers need the capacity to do this

"speculative engineering" and to compare that against the corporate R&D activities and their resulting products. Thus, for
example, much R&D in the automobile industry goes for cos-
metic changes. Some consumers value this, others do not. The
latter group has little capacity to tell automakers proactively
what they would buy. In fact, U.S. automakers, because they
failed to anticipate consumer demand for fuel-efficient cars
(among other reasons), have lost much of their market to the
Japanese. Lucas Aerospace workers, using their interpretation
of what consumers would want and should be provided, went
the next step. They identified how their factories could do the
retooling necessary to alter their product lines.

Another goal for anticipatory democracy in the marketplace
is well articulated, competing values applied to products. If Alvin Toffler is accurate in his depiction of the coming Third Wave,
conflict will become more frequent as society decentralizes and
diversifies. Thus, there may be several counterparts to Consumers Union, issuing its own *Consumer Reports*, judging R&D
possibilities and new products by different sets of values. In
this setting, a livelier democracy in the public and private sector would seek and benefit from the clash of values applied to
products in a technically sophisticated way.

OPTIONS?

How might this clash of well-informed consumers in a smarter
market—informed by technological possibilities, their relation
to values, and their impact on society—come about? If Toffler
is right, then much of this is already beginning to happen and
will continue to grow. What are some of the linkage mechanisms that would aid this, mechanisms that would link the
consumer and their values to the steering processes in the marketplace?

One set of mechanisms is the involvement of Consumers
Union (and other consumer-oriented groups) in "speculative
engineering," doing product comparisons on products not yet
produced. By formulating what R&D could provide, such groups
could monitor corporate R&D efforts. This type of speculation

is particularly necessary in the area of the communications revolution.

There is a technological imperative of great force that will affect every consumer's life over the next ten to twenty years. In the health area, for example, the communications revolution can provide tremendous benefits to consumers, as well as several serious problems (Bezold, 1981a). For example, we may have "hospitals-on-the-wrist" which diagnose and treat each of us in a very sophisticated and individualized manner. Yet computerized medical records, along with very precise genetic screening for disease, could be used by governments, employers, or others to invade our privacy. The communications revolution will provide local consumers groups with the opportunity to monitor quickly, easily, and cheaply the quality of services provided by health care providers. Yet the history of much communications technology is that it has placed more power in the hands of producers, advertisers, and marketers than it has given to consumers. This has occurred because the producer side of the market is organized and able to protect its interests. Additionally, the cost of evaluating and communicating about technologies can be very high. The new communications technologies may make it much cheaper. Also, the new technologies, such as computers, are decentralizing the capacity to evaluate various programs. James Turner (1983) has argued that the communications revolution could put much greater power in the hands of the consumers if even some consumer groups are willing to take advantage of the opportunities which home computer networks and other technologies provide. A small percentage of active consumers, evaluating products and disseminating their results, could be very significant.

In effect, consumers can turn their dollars into more conscious votes in the marketplace guided by a more assertive set of consumer-driven R&D evaluations.

Another approach is the generation of alternative scenarios of technological development by a government agency such as the Congressional Office of Technology Assessment, or as a component of scenarios of the United States. In 1983, congressmen Albert Gore and New Gingrich introduced legislation to develop a national foresight capability. Under this proposal, the

Executive Office of the President would develop alternative futures for the United States every four years, and Congress would
develop its own set of scenarios every two years. Alternatively,
or simultaneously, companies develop such scenarios and ex-
ercises for the public as part of a participatory market research
operation. There are a host of potential problems with reliance
on corporations for consumer scenarios, but if there were com-
petition in this area among companies and consumer groups,
as well as further development of corporate responsibility, this
would become more possible. For example, a recent life insurance industry report noted that

taken together, forces external to the private sector (including decentralization, self-reliance, and appropriate technology) are creating an
atmosphere where business leaders will be obligated to develop new
approaches to decisionmaking. At the same time, the public will expect these leaders to justify both their decision and the processes by
which they were reached. (American Council on Life Insurance, 1979:5).

There is also the possibility of forming consumer membership groups, like Consumers Union, with very specific values
or technological areas of specialization. Funding for some consumer activities could be developed through a checkoff at gro-
cery stores in a form similar to the election contribution checkoff option which taxpayers have. This is a model similar to the
Public Interest Research Groups generated by Ralph Nader,
though it would include a focus on the choices in research targeting and new product development as they are being made.

There have been a variety of experiments in "anticipatory
democracy" in the public sector which have pointed out the
possibility for citizens to take a more effective role in steering
the future of their communities. The same potential exists in
the private sector. This can occur through the development of
mechanisms for consumers and consumer groups to do "speculative engineering," to consider what new product lines they
need and would buy, as well as explore in advance the impacts
those new technologies would have on society. There are a host
of disincentives which hinder the development of these mech-

anisms, and they may not, in fact, occur. But they can, and there is some argument that they are a necessary part of larger trends in the evolution of industrial society into its next form. Policy scientists and others concerned with avoiding a technocratic society should focus some attention on these possibilities.

REFERENCES

American Council on Life Insurance 1979
> *Power and Decisions: Institutions in an Information Age*, Trend Analysis Program, TAP 18, Summer.

Baker, David E. 1978
> "State, Regional, and Local Experiments in Anticipatory Democracy: An Overview," in Clement Bezold, ed., *Anticipatory Democracy, People in the Politics of the Future.* (New York: Random House).

Bezold, Clement 1977
> *Strengthening Citizen Access and Governmental Accountability.* (Washington, D.C.: Exploratory Project for Economic Alternatives).

———, ed. 1978a
> *Anticipatory Democracy, People in the Politics of the Future.* (New York: Random House).

——— 1978b
> "Lucas Aerospace: The Workers Plan for Socially Useful Products," Bezold, *Anticipatory Democracy.*

——— 1979
> "Participation in Shaping the Future Alternative Futures for Citizen Education," *Futurics* 3:3:225–44.

——— 1980
> "Recombinant DNA, New Drugs, and Societal Choice," Foresight Seminar on Pharmaceutical Research and Development, Institute for Alternative Futures, May 20.

——— 1981a
> "Alternative Futures for Health Care: Emerging Issues and Society's Future," *National Journal*, May 30, pp. 998–1001.

——— 1981b
> *The Future of Pharmaceuticals: The Changing Environment for New Drugs.* (New York: Wiley).

Bezold, Clement, Christopher Jones, and Charles Wilson 1982
    "A Survey of Selected Citizen's Goals and Futures Projects,"
    Institute for Alternative Futures, Arlington, Virginia.
Coates, Joseph 1977
    "Life Patterns, Technology, and Political Institutions in Van C.
    Kussrow and Richard Baepler, eds. *Changing American Lifestyles*,
    Valparaiso, Indiana: Valparaiso University.
Collingridge, David 1980
    The Social Control of Technology. (New York: St. Martin's Press).
Ellis, William, and the editors of *The Futurist* 1977
    "Appropriate Technology," *The Futurist* 11:2:101–4.
Galbraith, John Kenneth 1967
    The New Industrial State. (Boston: Houghton Mifflin).
Gee, Robert E. 1977
    "Research Priorities: Allocation of Resources Among R&D Pro-
    grams," in Karl A. Stroetmann, ed., *Innovation, Economic Change
    and Technology Policies*. (Basel: Birkhauser Verlag).
George, Michael 1978
    "Which Future and Whose Future in Manufacturing Industry
    in the U.K.?" (Essex: Center for Alternative Industrial and
    Technological Systems of the North East London Polytechnic).
Henderson, Hazel 1978
    Creating Alternative Futures: The End of Economics. (New York:
    Berkley Publishing Company).
Lederman, Leonard L. 1977
    "Technological Innovation and Federal Government Policy—
    Research and Analysis of the Office of National R&D Assess-
    ment," in Karl A. Stroetmann, *Innovation, Economic Change and
    Technology Policies*. (Basel: Birkhauser Verlag).
Lindblom, Charles E. 1977
    Politics and Markets: The World's Political-Economic Systems. (New
    York: Basic Books).
Love, Sam 1977
    "The New Look of the Future," *The Futurist* 11:2:78–80.
McHale, John, and Magda Cordell McHale 1979
    "Basic Human Needs and Sustainable Growth," *The Futurist*
    13:18–27.
Mackenzie, MaryAnn 1981
    *Appropriate Community Technology—Some Criteria for Evaluating
    Projects*. U.S. Community Services Administration. (Washing-
    ton, D.C.: Government Printing Office).

Naisbitt, John 1982
Megatrends. (New York: Warner Books).
Editors of Rain 1977
Rainbook: Resources for Appropriate Technology. (New York: Schocken Books).
Rodale, Robert 1981
Our Next Frontier. (Emmaus, Pa.: Rodale Press).
Rosenbaum, Nelson M. 1978
"The Origins of Citizen Involvement in Federal Programs," in Bezold, *Anticipatory Democracy*.
Toffler, Alvin 1970
Future Shock. (New York: Random House).
——— 1978
"Introduction on Future-Conscious Politics," in Bezold, *Anticipatory Democracy*.
——— 1980
The Third Wave. (New York: Morrow).
Turner, James 1983
"Consumers, Computers, and Pharmaceuticals," in Clement Bezold, *Pharmaceuticals in the Year 2000*. (Alexandria, Va.: Institute for Alternative Futures).
Uhlmann, Luitpold 1977
"The Innovation Process in Industrialized Countries—Some Empirical Results," in Karl A. Stroetmann, *Innovation, Economic Change and Technology Policies*. (Basel: Birkhauser Verlag).
Utterback, James M., Thomas J. Allen, J. Herbert Holloman, and Marvin A. Sirbu, Jr., 1977
"The Process of Innovation in Five Industries in Europe and Japan," in Karl A. Stroetmann, *Innovation, Economic Change and Technology Policies*. (Basel: Birkhauser Verlag).
Verba, Sidney, and Norman H. Nie 1972
Participation in America: Political Democracy and Social Equality. (New York: Harper and Row).
Winner, Langdon 1977
Autonomous Technology: Technics-Out-of-Control as a Theme in Political Thought. (Cambridge, Mass.: MIT Press).

Part II

CURRENT PUBLIC DECISION-MAKING STRATEGIES IN THE UNITED STATES

5

Public Participation: Reflections on the California Energy Policy Experience

MICHAEL D. REAGAN AND VICTORIA LYNN FEDOR-THURMAN[1]

The research reported in this chapter unites a recent development (late 1960s onward) in the area of American political *processes*—that of citizen participation in administrative decision making—with a salient topic in substantive *policy*—energy. Because energy policy making is an area of great technological complexity, any study of participation in this area naturally relates also to the perennial problem of the citizen-expert relationship. Our specific focus is on the California Energy Commission (CEC), more formally designated the State Energy Resources Conservation and Development Commission. The methods are traditional: documentary research and personal interviews.

Verba and Nie (1972) devoted almost all of their attention to participation as traditionally exercised through electoral and political party activities. Government agencies were only then starting to invite public participation in administrative proceedings, often because of statutory requirements; yet this trend became almost a "movement" by the end of the 1970s (U.S. Advisory Commission on Intergovernmental Relations, 1979).[2] In light of some pulling back in the Reagan administration, public participation's programmatic high point to date consists of efforts to provide "intervenor funding," that is, public funds to enable representatives of the public to hire experts and to attend hearings (Aron, 1979). Literature describing and assessing participation in its new manifestation has begun to appear (for example, Langton, 1978; Rich and Rosenbaum, 1981; Kweit and Kweit, 1981), and this chapter is intended to contribute further in that context.

The overriding question we consider is the extent to which, and the manner in which, citizens may effectively contribute to the substantive content of policy, regardless of whatever other functions public participation might serve—for example, internal feelings of efficacy or acceptance of agency policy proposals (the goal that administrators presumably see as crucial). Disaggregated, this means investigating both the number and variety of public participants and attempting an evaluation necessarily subjective of the impact on policy. Has citizen participation, for example, affected CEC choices of "hard" or "soft" energy paths (Lovins, 1977; Morrison and Lodwick, 1981)? Has it led to policy changes? Has it reinforced agency policy trends? Or has it been meaningless?

A second focus developed as our research proceeded: to explore perceptions of the actual and potential roles of an official Public Adviser. Operating with limited resources, we concentrated on California's major agency for basic energy policy development, the CEC, whose entire focus concerns energy (as distinguished from the California Public Utilities Commission [PUC], whose jurisdiction also includes regulated transportation and communication activities). The Energy Commission performs such major functions as forecasting and planning for future energy demand and supply, power plant siting, and sponsoring research on alternative energy sources. It constituted a particularly interesting choice for participation research because it also has a statutory Public Adviser (P.A.) with specific responsibilities for the enhancement of public participation in the affairs of the agency.

The CEC was established by statute (Warren-Alquist Act, Public Resources Code 25100 et seq.) in 1974 and has been one of the best supported financially of energy policy bodies among the fifty states. Its policy responsibilities are shared with other state agencies, notably the PUC. This latter agency operates at what one might call a lower level of abstraction in that it deals primarily with the actualities of energy "here and now," although matters such as rate structures obviously are a part of planning for the future. Furthermore, because it directly regulates rates, it is on the "front line" of consumer concerns regarding gas and electric (and phone) costs. Such concerns increasingly elicit public participation rather strongly focused on the particular simple objective of lower rates. Given the PUC's significant role, our study was extended to include some basic interviews in that agency, but only far enough to provide some speculative points of comparison.

DESCRIPTIVE FINDINGS

Given the statutory presence of a Public Adviser and the great openness to public participation (which our interviews make clear existed in the California Energy Commission), the greatest surprise of our study was the insignificant quantity of public participation. This is apparent, for example, in the biennial report process.

Legislatively mandated biennial reports by the CEC constitute the most basic energy policy-making documents developed within California state government. These reports enjoy a near-monopoly on publicly generated, publicly available analyses of future energy demand and supply alternatives, as well as on policy recommendations that may place policy issues on the agendas of the legislature, the Public Utilities Commission, the private utilities, and the citizenry. A very substantial CEC staff develops the information and analyses contained in the biennial reports, extensive consultation is held with industrial groups—such as oil companies and public utilities—and extensive hearings are held.

For Biennial Report III (BR III), titled *Energy Tomorrow* (CEC, 1981), the CEC held fifty-four sets of public hearings. At only fourteen did members of the public participate in some fashion. At these fourteen sessions, participants totaled twenty-one, of whom about half were individual private citizens and the rest were representatives of various organized groups. BR IV proceedings (November 1981 through August 1982), on the topic

Securing California's Energy Future (CEC, 1982a), produced even less citizen participation: 23 sessions without public comment, five with. One explanation for the sparse turnout may be that tight budget restrictions necessitated holding most of the hearings in Sacramento. This location does not provide easy access to the major population areas of California.

CEC records show that BR III hearings included public testimony by representatives of three major resource protection groups (Sierra Club, Environmental Defense Fund, Natural Resources Defense Council), some more localized grass-roots organizations (Ecology Action of the Mid-Peninsula, Coalition of Communities Against Power Lines, Community Action Network of San Diego), a university professor of electrical engineering, a retired professor in the field of engine technology, and individual citizens. One of the latter spoke for the use of grain for gasohol, another in favor of biomass; one was concerned with smog, and another advocated use of electric cars. BR IV participation included representatives of five public interest groups, plus three individual citizens.

The policy "line" of the CEC in Biennial Report III was a heavy emphasis on conservation and alternative technologies, such as renewables and cogeneration, stressing strongly the importance of reducing reliance upon expensive and disruptable oil supplies. The commission clearly opted for the soft path to efficiency and conservation, as opposed to the building of more capital-intensive, centralized coal or nuclear plants. In BR III, the CEC described its changing focus as being a transition from the early days of 1974–75 when the major issue was perceived as the need for new power plants to meet steadily growing electrical demand. The commission suggested that a turning point was the 1978 proceeding on a proposed Sundesert nuclear plant. Commentators, including the Public Adviser, have said that interest group pressures were partially responsible for the negative Sundesert outcome. If so, that was because of the intensity or persuasive quality of presentations, rather than because of numbers or variety of public participants, since a quick perusal of the master log for the Sundesert proceedings (CEC Docket No. 76-N01-2) showed a pattern of public participation not substantially different from that reported above regarding

BR III. It therefore seems that one cannot credit public participation with having played a major role overall in leading the Energy Commission to its present pro-soft position because it seems that is where the commission had been heading anyway.

Discussions in 1982 with both staff members and commissioners indicated a substantial agency consensus on the policy directions indicated in BR III: conservation-consciousness, concern with environmental protection, encouragement for local development of renewable energy sources, and generally implicit disdain for the traditional scenario that sees ever-rising power demand as synonymous with economic growth and the good society. Such views might be regarded as a reaction to disruptive economic events—the induced rise in oil prices, the deregulation of oil and gas prices in federal policy, demand reductions related both to those factors and to economic recession, the fall from favor of nuclear power, and the inability of utilities to put together the tremendous quantities of capital required to build traditional centralized plants. Perhaps these events have all had much more to do with the positions taken by the CEC than any conceivable amount of public participation might have engendered.

Although the biennial report process is the most important activity of the CEC from a broad public viewpoint, the fact is that the large majority of CEC projects on which hearings are held are much more specific and particularistic than the biennial report proceedings. An example are hearings held on the Residential Conservation Service (RCS), a federally mandated program for encouraging residential consumers to install conservation equipment and utilize solar energy. It was the CEC's task to establish a California plan for the RCS. In doing so, it held a number of hearings and utilized an advisory committee. Again, individual citizens, or ad hoc citizen groups, were not present in significant numbers, but representatives of various economic interests related to residential conservation, actually or potentially, were very much in evidence as a specific kind of "public." For example, participants in hearings on the RCS included the Mendocino Solar Association, Western Sun (an industrial group), a public solar coalition, and—most signifi-

cantly—representatives of various community-based organizations (CBOs) that wanted "a piece of the action" in the con-
ducting of home energy audits. According to one of the
commissioners, the CBOs' presence was indeed effective (partially, however, because of a staff member's direct contact with
a number of CBOs, rather than because of spontaneous appearances at hearings). As a result, strong language was written into the RCS for the utilities to use CBOs in their audit
programs. If one defines the public as consisting of small busi-
nesspersons, manufacturers, and installers of solar and other
conservation equipment, then the public was well represented
in the RCS hearings and through an advisory committee established for the 1982 RCS revision process. Even the "individual
citizen" generally turned out to be a small businessperson with
a gripe about a policy that was already in place, such as an
insulation contractor unhappy with RCS regulations. The
mythical disinterested citizen contributing his or her thoughts
for the common good was not in evidence.

Yet another level of greater specificity is reached with what
has been until recently (when new power plans have slowed
down) one of the major activities of the CEC, power plant siting. Siting cases involve a two-stage process. First is a notice
of intent, and later is an application for certification—the first
being on the general concept and need, and the second being
on specific site and construction details. In hearings on such
cases, one approaches questions not simply of general policy
but of the particular location of particular kinds of equipment
having particular anticipatable environmental impacts. For example, if a coal or nuclear plant is under consideration, the
environmental protection and safety problems loom large immediately; one need only mention Diablo Canyon.

No matter what the source of power, the placement of abov-
eground transmission lines is a matter of both economic and
aesthetic impact. Perhaps typical of the kinds of concerns expressed, but atypical in the great extent of public participation
and concern, is the case of Geisers Unit 16, a geothermal power
augmentation on which hearings were held in the spring of
1980. Individual participants expressed the following types of
concerns: the height of the transmission lines that would be

run near roads; the diameter of the towers scheduled to go through villages; possible effects of power loss in the lines passing near homes; why the lines were not to be placed underground. Also, a homeowners' association expressed concern about creek pollution from the geothermal residue. On this matter, and others like it, there was much more public participation of an individual citizen and ad hoc neighborhood group character than we found in the hearings on the larger policy questions.

A primary proposition is suggested: the more closely the matter touches on the personal life of an individual, the more likely the individual is to take the effort to participate in the hearing process; conversely, the more general and abstract the policy content, the less likely one is to find individual public participation. For a societal viewpoint, this may mean that participation is weakest where it should be strongest. A second proposition is that participation by the large, professionalized interest groups, such as the Sierra Club and Natural Resources Defense Council, runs in the other direction: they are increasingly likely to be involved the more the matter involves general policy.

Another way of stating this gradation from general to particular and from abstract to concrete is to put it in terms of a difference between general policy and specific decision. In this sense, using the California agencies as examples, one might say that CEC agenda items tend to be on the policy side while PUC matters tend to be on the specific decision side, at least in the sense that rate determination cases have an obvious and immediate effect upon individuals. Within the context of the PUC, however, it might be rejoined that rate structure cases (that is, those that determine the differential portions of the total rate imposition to be born by various categories of users) are more like a general policy. At least, their effects are not as immediately discernible or understandable by the general public as those concerning the rates themselves.

We did not examine PUC documents to ascertain the numbers and the types of public participation involved. However, the California press gives a clear impression, particularly in the last couple of years, that participation in PUC cases differs from that in CEC hearings insofar as there is a much greater tendency toward ad hoc personal involvement in the former. For example, consider the many hundreds of consumers who protested announced rate increases for Pacific Gas and Electric in the spring of 1982. Greater participation is also cited for groups focused on rates as such, rather than more general policy questions. Most notable among these groups in TURN (Toward Utility Rate Normalization). Another organized group, purported to have had a significant impact in furthering the lifeline rate concept, is the Citizen Action League (CAL). However, CAL has been described as a staff-led organization using the lifeline issue as a device to build membership for a variety of purposes, and this would hardly qualify as a "grass-roots" citizen organization in the basic sense of that term (Anderson, 1981:144–56).

Perceptions of Commissioners

Having reviewed the participants, let us look now at the perceptions of CEC commissioners regarding public participation generally.[3] One of the commissioners, stating that he very strongly and without reservation supported the ideal of public participation as embedded in the Warren-Alquist Act, nevertheless quickly went on to say that the reality diverges considerably from the ideal. From his view, public participation was not effective when a general policy issue was up for settlement, but was effective "when someone's ox was gored." This "gored ox" concept of the conditions for effective citizen participation was widely agreed to among the commissioners. Most citizens, pointed out another commissioner, could not afford the time to participate in commission proceedings and generally assumed that government agencies were handling problems adequately. He thought that representatives of interest groups do a good job of representing various public points of view, if only because so many such representatives participate in the process. For this commissioner, the important point was less the actual extent of public participation than the fact that there exists an open process that allows for public participation whenever the public wants to bother to participate. He also thought it important that in CEC proceedings a commissioner is present to hear the tones of voice of the speakers and witnesses and to take note of the body language of those testifying and of the audience members. (This view was shared by the Public Adviser).

The activities of public interest groups and even of mass public demonstrations are important, he believed, in letting the commissioners ascertain the public's depth of concern on a particular issue. Another commissioner stated that the most important goal was to get the commission "out there" in order to gain legitimacy in the public eye by confronting the public directly. He believed that local hearings increase public participation when advance work is well done regarding publicity and dissemination of information on which members of the public can base a good grasp of the issues before they come to speak.

The commissioners generally felt that spontaneous individual participation is not likely to provide effective representation in the more technical areas. Instead, some commissioners have been strong advocates of the use of carefully formulated advisory groups to bolster participation in areas where such involvement might not otherwise effectively occur. The advisory commission for RCS has been mentioned, and there has been one for the building conservation standards programs. Both BR III and BR IV processes have had advisory committees. The committee for BR IV included representatives from individual manufacturing concerns, the California Manufacturers Association, the University of California, the Sierra Club, the Natural Resources Defense Council, Standard Oil of California, Southern California Edison, the Sacramento Municipal Utility District, the Bank of America, a black female community activist, a Chicano group, and state legislative committees. The committee appeared to be fairly broad in the interests represented, with the exception that all members were from northern California. This, however, may be largely unavoidable, especially if one is not to restrict membership to the wealthy, inasmuch as budgetary policy in 1982 did not permit reimbursement of travel expenses to members of CEC advisory committees.

Only one commissioner indicated significant qualification regarding the importance of public participation. This individual suggested, for example, that the commissioners are themselves sensitive to the needs of low-income persons, and therefore the lack of attendance by low-income persons at meetings does not mean that their concerns are not being addressed. In his view, the de facto representation of interests is more important than direct input.

The commissioners as a group seem to have a positive attitude toward the role of the various interest groups that appear most often before them, seeing these groups as surrogates for individual citizen participation. However, they did note that the pattern of active groups did not adequately represent two segments of the public: consumers as such and the low-income population.

Role of the Public Adviser

Given this underrepresentation, let us now examine the role of the Public Adviser in statute as perceived by the incumbent at the time of the interviews in mid-1982 and as evaluated by commissioners and others.

By statute (Sections 25222 and 25519 of the California Public Resources Code and Sections 2551-2557 of the Administrative Code), Title 20 defines the overall job of the Public Adviser as being "to ensure that full and adequate participation by the members of the public is secured in the commission's proceedings." The Adviser is to accomplish this by "(1) advising the public how to participate fully in the commission's proceedings, thereby providing the commission with the most comprehensive record feasible in those proceedings; and (2) advising the commission on the measures it should employ to ensure open consideration of public participation in its proceedings." The P.A. is specifically prohibited from representing any members of the public or from advocating "any substantive position on issues before the commission," although he or she may advocate "points of procedure" that might "improve public participation." The administrative code further spells out that the Adviser shall be available to any member of the public with an interest in participating in the commission's proceedings and shall advise members of the public of ways that they might make their participation most effective. This includes advising when an attorney or expert witness might be necessary or helpful to participation, assisting members of the public in obtaining access to the public records of the commission, referring members of the public to commission staff for information, organizing the appearances of public participants, and soliciting the participation of the members of the public whose participation the Adviser deems necessary or desirable. Those are the lines of formal authority and their limits, but what is actually done?

The 1982 P.A. was the third person in years to hold that position. The first Adviser got involved in some controversy over secret meetings, and the second, as perceived by her successor, followed a "due process" paperwork approach: seeing that everything was done by the book so that the commission would not be subject to further criticism. The second P.A. did try to obtain intervenor funding and to enlarge the operation; the files contain copies of her unsuccessful memoranda.

The 1982 P.A. (a Latino female) defined her own special niche as that of outreach: stimulating witnesses, traveling about to get input and make the CEC's activities known, suggesting types of witnesses to the commissioners, and suggesting topics to potential witnesses. In her budget requests (also unsuccessful) she tried to get intervenor funding and to obtain resources for opening a Los Angeles field office so that there could be greater participation for persons not residing in the Sacramento area. She perceived an important part of her role was to remind commissioners of their duties when they or staff offices reporting to them were, for example, stifling participation by not providing enough time or not encouraging an adequate mix of witnesses.

Herself a minority attorney, the P.A. told an interviewer that she attempted to point out the positions and viewpoints of the underrepresented. She believed that the face value of a broadly representative group on the advisory committee was useful, that it was good to sensitize the commmission to see black and brown persons (the staff becoming sensitized as well), and that minority representation was of symbolic importance. She indicated that an aggressive Public Adviser's office, which follows up inquiries with calls and functions as a liaison to obtain information for potential participants, alleviates some of the public's discouragement over the difficulties of participating. An example was cited of an individual who was helped in getting the CEC to act as a partner in his wind farm venture, thus smoothing his path in obtaining necessary permits. The Public Adviser indicated that she left environmental concerns to the Environmental Defense Fund and the Sierra Club, freeing herself to put her time, resources, and expertise into helping those who did not have the resources to be effective on their own.

This Public Adviser saw a number of goals for participation, including actual policy impact, legitimation of agency policies, and building of support for CEC policies. She disagreed with the "gored ox" concept to some extent, arguing that it is reasonable that public participation should be increased when the results of a decision affect someone personally. Moreover, she contended that the siting and construction of a geothermal plant and its power lines may affect water quality and is a policy problem, not just a matter of someone's ox being gored. On the other hand, she did suggest that a problem facing participation in policy is that the material is "just too complex, too technical for the citizens to understand." In fact, the Public Adviser's staff also has problems with some of the technical materials "because [the staff] is not composed of technocrats."

An issue that surfaces from time to time is that of whether the P.A. should be a neutral facilitator for public participation or an advocate for the underrepresented. As quoted above, the law embraces the neutral facilitator view. The then-incumbent P.A., on the other hand, would have preferred the freedom to take positions on issues. Since one always has more to do than time in which to do it, presumably any Public Adviser can place some emphasis of orientation where he or she wants through selection of opportunities presented.

Among the commissioners, there was a difference of view. One stated vehemently that the office of the P.A. presently is "a eunuch" because of the legal constraints that are imposed. This commissioner believed that the administrative code should have stricken the clause that forbids the P.A. to take a substantive position. Another argued definitely against this role for the

P.A. A third stated ambiguously that the neutrality is helpful on some issues, but that letting the P.A. be an advocate
would be helpful for unrepresented or underrepresented persons.

More generally, all of the commissioners appeared to be
strongly committed to openness of administrative proceedings
and maximizing opportunity for public participation, and they
saw the office of the Public Adviser as useful and facilitating
participation. They saw obstacles of time, information, and financial resources as standing in the way of effective individual
citizen participation, and one argued that a function of the P.A.
is to help to overcome some of those drawbacks, particularly
by providing adequate information and timely notice of meetings. Another would like to have added resources to the office
of the P.A. to enable it to provide professional advice to citizens. Yet another viewed the role of the P.A. as one of ensuring that everyone who has an interest in a proceeding is informed on the forthcoming issues and is encouraged to
participate, thus stressing the neutral facilitator role.

In the view of one senior member of the CEC staff, the extent of general public participation was somewhat less by 1982
than in earlier years, partly because former public interest group
representatives are now in the state government. The major
public interest groups, he indicated, maintain a close level of
contact with CEC staff on a continuing basis and therefore do
not need to appear formally very often in the open public hearings. Overall, this person saw the mandated openness as a major asset and outside pushes as significant in a number of instances, such as the Sundesert nuclear plant, the influence of
the city of Davis on building efficiency standard policies, and
the efforts of a public interest group in suggesting a new method
of demand forecasting that improved on what the oil companies and utilities had been doing previously. In fact, he suggested that there is a continuing need for the groups to press
the CEC because there might not be enough internal imagina-
tion. In this connection, he cited the Natural Resources Defense Council (NRDC) and the concept of a second generation
program in regard to refrigerator efficiency in the energy appli-
ance efficiency program.

The Interest Group Perspective

This, of course, leads to the perspective of interest group representatives interviewed for this project. Confirming one of the points made above, a representative of a major group stated that "informal staff contacts are the most effective way to get things done" and that his group was not generally a formal participant in proceedings.

We might note, without fully developing the point, that several persons interviewed, from both the CEC and PUC, asserted that the agency staffs constitute an important link to the public and even provide a kind of implicit public representation. The staff, so runs the argument, does not work in a vacuum. Staffers are influenced by news reports and other external stimuli that sensitize them to the environmental concerns of the public, as well as to the economic development concerns of business and union organizations. To the extent that staff (and commissioners themselves, for that matter) internalize the values of segments of the public not directly represented at hearings, a kind of virtual representation exists. The perennial problem with this concept is, of course, its accidental quality: the luck of the draw determines which values the staff will itself embody and with which unrepresented groups it will identify.

Representatives of two major groups express fairly strong views on CEC-PUC differences in openness to public participation. Both thought that the PUC and CEC should expand their use of citizen advisory committees and said that the PUC needs a Public Adviser.[4] One indicated that the CEC is generally more informal in its hearings, saying that he felt "less intimidated" before the CEC than before the PUC. The legal procedure and the fact that administrative law judges (ALJs) preside at PUC hearings made it difficult, it was said, for nonattorneys to adjust, in comparison with the CEC procedures in which commissioners preside in an informal manner. Even regarding information made available to the public, whether individuals or groups, a possibly significant difference was pointed out: the CEC does not charge for any of its information or annual reports (and in our experience the agency in fact has a commendably vigorous public information program), while the PUC may charge up to $200 a year for its agendas and calendars, which are required if one is to keep informed of what is going on and in which hearings one might wish to participate. Also, the interest group representatives point out that the PUC has no commissioner at its hearings, except for the very large ones, thus getting their information filtered through the ALJs. A senior PUC staff member, while arguing that lack of knowledge and expertise on the part of the public is the major obstacle to effective participation, acknowledged that the "court-type hearings" may make it more difficult for the public to participate than when a less legal framework is utilized. Another PUC staff member said that anyone whose group is well organized and has resources and expertise will have some influence, but that a commissioner does not ordinarily attend any hearings is a weakness. This person also suggested that a commissioner should be appointed to represent the consumers, while another staff member favored a totally independent citizen advisory board.

One senior, longtime PUC official presented a different picture. In correspondence, he has pointed out that some PUC documents are free and that those for which charges are made are available for perusal at nineteen commission offices throughout the state. He also pointed to the Consumer Affairs Branch, whose multitudinous daily contacts with consumers present the PUC with "tangible reactions" and feedback "as to what is happening at the grass-roots level." We mention these varied perceptions only to suggest a range of possible factors and to indicate that differing organizational functions and structures may affect the handling of participation.

We have now presented our findings and summarized the perceptions of public participation, its potential and its limitations, as seen from the perspectives of commissioners, staff members, and interest group representatives. In the next section we attempt a brief analysis of these findings in light of conceptualizations of propositions about public participation, and we ask a few tentative questions about policy directions.

INTERPRETATION

Rationales for Participation

Two different reasons for increased citizen participation (a term we use interchangeably with public participation) are found in the literature, and both may be accurate. The first points to a mix of institutional developments: the decline of traditional mediating institutions between citizens and government, especially the decline of the national political parties; the rise of bureaucratic decision making, as discretion given to administrators by legislative bodies has increased; and the widespread publicity about governmental problems that the mass media provide (Langton, 1978:6–7). A quite different explanation lies in the more amorphous realm of changes in perceived public values. From this viewpoint, the recent expansion of participation in the realm of administrative decision making can be compared with "previous surges of democratic values during the Jacksonian and Progressive eras" (Nelson M. Rosenbaum, in Langton, 1978:48). Whichever set of reasons may be more accurate (and there is no incompatibility between them), it is certainly a matter of fact that citizen participation and administrative proceedings have increased substantially, with much official underpinning in the form of regulations requiring participation as part of various kinds of decision making.

In addition to a duality of rationales behind public participation, we need also to take note of duality in function and in strategies. Citizen participation, as seen by citizen groups, has the functions of serving as a control mechanism over government and of making contributions to the substantive content of policy. From the viewpoint of administrative agencies, the literature suggests that the major functions are probably more often seen as the building of support for agency programs, defusing opposition, and co-opting potentially "difficult" citizens or groups of citizens. Again, these are not mutually exclusive, but they do complicate one's assessment of what should be expected from public participation and how it may best be pursued. In terms of strategies that political leadership may pursue with regard to soliciting citizen participation, the analysis made by Verba and Nie (1972) provides the best expression of the classic dilemma. Political leaders, they say, can ask citizens, or a representative sample thereof, about their policy preferences by polling; or, they can wait until citizens come to them to present their points of view (which is roughly what nonvoting, nonpolling participation means, in terms of actual practices). The contrast they describe between these strategies is worth quoting:

The polling strategy covers the entire population and seeks out the inarticulate. But . . . it records both the opinions of the thoughtful and the opinions of those who have given the problem little thought; it equates the intensely concerned with the citizen for whom the problem may not have existed until the pollster showed up at his door. The participation method records only the views of those who have views; and takes into account the intensity of opinions, and it eliminates the "noise" from a mass population that has little to say on the subject. In so doing, this method leaves a large portion (indeed often an overwhelming portion) of the population unheard from. It gives differential access to social groups—often the special interest rather than the general but less intense interest. Which technique reflects and which distorts it? The question is important but unanswerable. Each technique elicits a reality of sorts. (Verba and Nie, 1972:268–69)

If one assumes—as we believe many of those we talked to in the course of this research implicitly do—that public participation, to have a legitimate impact, should represent the general public fairly (that is, bear some factual relationship to the actual distribution of interest and views among the public), then the shortcomings to which Verba and Nie refer in the participation method constitute a strong criticism of the adequacy of most participations. Certainly, our findings regarding the CEC bear out the Verba and Nie description and therefore raise questions about the meaning of public participation as practiced in relationship to the CEC and perhaps point to some of the functions most needed to be performed by a Public Adviser. One might also note among these basic considerations that even when the "special interests" are those represented by the "public interest groups," many of these are what might best be called staff groups rather than mass-membership groups, have oligarchic internal structures, and therefore raise additional questions about the extent to which group participation can be said to equal citizen participation. On the other hand, even if the public interest group picture is not one of 100 percent democracy, what it does accomplish is what Schattschneider (1960) suggested as a necessary step in reaching a public interest, namely, to enlarge the scope of conflict so that a broader range of views has to be heard before a decision is made, especially in a pressure system in which many interests tend not to be well organized.

Categories of Participation

Public or citizen participation can be subcategorized in many ways, not all of which need be reviewed for present applied purposes. However, at least a few broad distinctions relevant to participation in general do appear to be significantly related to our findings regarding participation in California energy policy making. Specifically, a distinction often needs to be made between participation with regard to *policy development* as opposed to participation in *individual case decisions*, with the latter not involved in establishing future rules to apply to other cases (which is one definition of policy). Broad policy can also be distinguished from the details of programs intended to implement the policies. For example, the concept of a residential conservation service would be seen as a broad policy in which the values to be served are as important as the technical matters needing resolution. However, the particulars of how the program is to be administered—in terms of the role of utilities as bankers, the rate structure distribution of the costs of energy audits, etc.—are matters in which the value preferences of the general public may have less relevance than more technical input.

Similarly, we believe that participation efforts in energy policy making could be enhanced if thoughtful analysis were given to the procedural distinctions that might follow from recognizing more explicitly the differences among the various participants: individuals as individuals; ad hoc local community groups that coalesce briefly around one particular decision and then

are likely to disperse; economic interest groups, whether producers or consumers; single interest groups (for example, California Tea Party or TURN) as compared with multi-interest
groups (for example, the Sierra Club, California Chambers of
Commerce); and staff groups operating largely independently
on a membership, as compared with those in which the leadership is clearly reflecting the values of a mass membership.

In the materials we covered, we found very little participation by individuals as individuals and in fact have some doubt
about the value of even that small amount in most instances.
When it came to the broadest kind of policy, such as the biennial reports, most of the group participation was of one particular variety, namely public interest groups of a staff- more than
a mass-membership character. Such groups plus economic interest groups, particularly those of producers, participated in
program development at a level where decisions would be made
having a directly predictable impact on the use of certain types
of equipment sales or certain types of services.

Public Participation and Public Representation

The clearest finding is that public participation of the kinds
we found does not mean representation of the general public.
Let us hasten to say that we make this statement as a matter
of fact, not as a criticism; we have some real doubt that public
participation in administrative policy making through appearances at hearings or the submission of written testimony or
recommendations can ever be "representative" of the electorate. The important question, therefore, is how hard should a
commission try—how much of its resources should it use in
trying—simply to broaden the number of individual participants, or ad hoc groups of participants, for the sake of claiming
a larger element of participation? The author of a policy analysis textbook (Wildavsky, 1979:253) says this of citizen participation in policy development: "In order for citizens to participate in the operation of policy, they would have to understand
what is in it for them, recognize the differences between small
and large changes (so as what to know whether and how much
participation was worthwhile), and be involved continuously

so that they could learn from experience." Indiscriminate stim-
ulation of those who have little knowledge and few opinions
about energy policy would not seem to be a strategy of great
public value, although there is a school of thought (without
much operational evidence behind it) which holds that individual participation is "good for the soul" in the sense of developing feelings of efficacy and in providing an education in citizenship.

Feasible Goals for Participation

One of the goals that public participation can sometimes serve
is a goal that the CEC commissioners and senior staff seem
honestly to welcome and which is often the major goal of public interest groups. That goal is the broadening of the range of
ideas, knowledge, and viewpoints that are brought to bear in
the development of substantive policy content. NRDC's demand forecasting methodology and the Environmental Defense
Fund's economic analysis of an environmentally dangerous coal-
power project are perhaps good examples of the positive substantive content sometimes provided through the participation
process. Our interviews also suggest that carefully structured
advisory committees may be an important mode of participation oriented specifically toward the provision of improved
substantive content, rather than protesting decisions made (say,
PUC rate decisions) or simply expressing a value preference for
decentralized energy supply sources at a public hearing. By
"carefully structured" we do not mean a committee structured
simply with an eye to political realities and the co-optation of
groups that might otherwise make negative noises; rather, we
mean to emphasize selection of members in terms of the
knowledge-based contributions they can make, either in a technical sense (engineering, economics, etc.) or in terms of knowledge of political feasibility as defined by major group reactions
to various policy options.

Participation and Technological Complexity

Finally, our review of CEC documents and the interviews
reinforce the unsurprising observation that public participation

faces severe and sometimes crippling obstacles in the form of complexity of issues (that is, the number of different facets to be considered and among which trade-offs must be determined), the technical nature of many of the issues involved, the inadequacy of information reaching the affected public, and, of course, the problem of inadequate resources in time and money for participation, particularly by individuals but to some extent shared by many of the groups that might wish to act as intervenors. At this point, we may conclude our brief effort to develop some descriptive information and some analytic perspectives by pointing out that these last observations suggest that citizen participation in energy matters might, in additional work, be further illuminated by comparison with other technology-democracy interaction studies—for example, Schwing and Albers (1980), Caldwell et al. (1976), Primack and von Hippel (1974), and Abrams and Primack (1980). A final speculative proposition might be that while organized public interest groups can (and do) make substantive policy constitutions, the primary role of the individual citizen facing a technologically complex agency may be to show, in A. D. Lindsay's classic phrase (Lindsay, 1943), "where the shoe pinches."

NOTES

1. We wish to acknowledge research grant 81–196–4000 from the U.C. Appropriate Technology Program and supplementary funding from the Energy Sciences Program, University of California, Riverside.

2. We speculate that the simultaneous rise of public interest groups (Walker, 1981) may not be entirely accidental. Both may be manifestations of a larger trend toward the development of new linkages between citizens and government.

3. Material is from interviews, except as otherwise indicated.

4. Legislation enacted in the summer of 1982 in fact mandated that the PUC appoint a Public Adviser, beginning January 1, 1983.

REFERENCES

Abrams, Nancy E., and Joe R. Primack 1980
    "The Public and Technological Decisions," *Bulletin of the Atomic Scientists* 36:6:44–48.

Anderson, Douglas D. 1981
    Regulatory Politics and Electric Utilities. (Boston: Auburn House).
Aron, Joan B. 1979
    "Intergovernmental Politics of Energy," *Policy Analysis* 5:451–71.
Caldwell, Lynton, D., Lester Hayes, and Ian MacWhirter 1976
    Citizens and the Environment. (Bloomington: Indiana University Press).
California Energy Commission 1981
    Moving Toward Security: Strategies for Reducing California's Vulnerability to Energy Shortages. Draft Report. (Sacramento: California Energy Commission).
—— 1982a
    Securing California's Energy Future. Biennial Report IV. Draft. (Sacramento: California Energy Commission, October).
—— 1982b
    Government Behavior in an Oil Crisis: An Analysis of the Rand Emergency Simulation. (Sacramento: California Energy Commission, June).
Colglazier, E. William, ed. 1982
    The Politics of Nuclear Waste. (New York: Pergamon Press).
Committee on Nuclear and Alternative Energy Systems (CONAES), National Research Council 1979
    Energy in Transition: 1985–2010. (Wahington, D.C.: National Academy of Sciences).
Ebinger, Charles K., et al. 1982
    The Critical Link: Energy and National Security in the 1980s. Report of the Georgetown University Project on Energy and National Security. (Cambridge, Mass.: Ballinger).
Goodwin, Craufurd D., ed. 1981
    Energy Policy in Perspective. (Washington, D.C.: Brookings Institution).
Hall, Timothy A., Irwin L. White, and Steven C. Ballard 1978
    "Western States and National Energy Policy," *American Behavioral Scientist* 22:191–212.
Kweit, Mary Grisez, and Robert W. Kweit 1981
    Implementing Citizen Participation in a Bureaucratic Society. (New York: Praeger Special Studies).
Landsberg, H. H., et al. 1979
    Energy: The Next Twenty Years. (Cambridge, Mass.: Ballinger).
Langton, Stuart, ed. 1978
    Citizen Participation in America. (Lexington, Mass.: Lexington Books).

Lindsay, A. D. 1943
   The Modern Democratic State. (London: Oxford University Press).
Lovins, Amory B. 1977
   Soft Energy Paths. (Cambridge, Mass.: Ballinger, 1977; Harper
   Colophon, ed., 1979).
Morrison, Denton E., and Dora G. Lodwick 1981
   "The Social Impacts of Soft and Hard Energy Systems," in Jack
   Hollander, ed., *Annual Review of Energy.* (Ann Arbor, Mich.:
   Annual Reviews), pp. 357–78.
National Energy Policy Plan 1981
   "Securing America's Energy Future." (Washington, D.C.: U.S.
   Department of Energy).
Noam, Eli M. 1980
   "The Interaction of Federal Deregulation and State Regulation,"
   Hofstra Law Review 9:195–210.
Primack, Joel, and Frank von Hippel 1974
   Advice and Dissent: Scientists in the Political Arena. (New York:
   Basic Books).
Reagan, Michael D. 1963
   The Managed Economy. (New York: Oxford University Press).
——— 1969
   Science and the Federal Patron. (New York: Oxford University
   Press).
——— 1972
   The New Federalism. (New York: Oxford University Press; rev.
   ed. with John G. Sanzone, 1981).
——— 1982a
   "Energy: Government Policy or Market Result?" Paper deliv-
   ered at the American Political Science Association meetings,
   Denver, Colo.
——— 1982b
   "Public Participation in California Energy Policy-Making." Re-
   port to the University of California Appropriate Technology
   Program, U.C. Davis.
——— 1983
   "The Federalism Factor in Energy Policy," in Max Neiman and
   Barbara J. Burt, eds. *The Social Constraints on Energy Policy Implementation.* (Lexington, Mass.: Lexington Books).
Rich, Richard C., and Walter A. Rosenbaum, eds. 1981
   Citizen Participation in Public Policy, symposium in *Journal of Ap-
   plied Behavioral Science* 17:4:439–614.

Schattschneider, E. E. 1960
   The Semi-Sovereign People. (New York: Holt, Rinehart, and Winston).
Schurr, S. H., ed. 1979
   Energy in America's Future: The Choices Before Us. Report of the National Energy Strategies Project. (Baltimore, Md.: Johns Hopkins for Resources for the Future).
Schwing, Richard C., and Walter A. Albers, Jr., eds. 1980
   Societal Risk Assessment: How Safe Is Safe Enough? (New York: Plenum).
Spangler, Miller B. 1980
   Federal-State Cooperation in Nuclear Power Plant Licensing. (Washington, D.C.: U.S. Nuclear Regulatory Commission, Office of Nuclear Reactor Regulation, NU REG-0398).
Stobaugh, Robert, and Daniel Yergin 1979
   Energy Future: Report Energy Project at the Harvard Business School. (New York: Random House, 1979; rev. ed., Ballantine Books, 1980).
U.S. Advisory Commission on Intergovernmental Relations 1979
   Citizen Participation in the American Federal System Report A-73. (Washington, D.C.: ACIR).
——— 1981a
   An Agenda for American Federalism. Report A-86. (Washington, D.C.: ACIR, June).
——— 1981b
   The Condition of Contemporary Federalism: Conflicting Theories and Collapsing Constraints. Report A-78. (Washington, D.C.: ACIR, August).
Verba, Sidney, and Norman H. Nie 1972
   Participation in America: Political Democracy and Social Equality. (New York: Harper and Row).
Von Hippel, Frank 1981
   "The Emperor's New Clothes—1981," *Physics Today* 34:7:34–41.
Walker, Jack L. 1981
   "The Origins and Maintenance of Interest Groups in Ameica." Paper read at the American Political Science Association meetings, New York.
Wilbanks, Thomas J. 1981
   "Planning for Energy Emergencies." Draft paper. (Oak Ridge, Tenn.: Oak Ridge National Laboratory).
——— 1981
   "Planning for Energy Emergencies." Working paper prepared for the Committee on Behavioral and Social Aspects of Energy

Consumption and Production, National Academy of Sciences/National Research Council, March.

Wildavsky, Aaron 1979
Speaking Truth to Power: The Art and Craft of Policy Analysis. (Boston: Little, Brown).

6

Procedures for Citizen Involvement in Environmental Policy: An Assessment of Policy Effects

MARCUS E. ETHRIDGE

The image of citizen participation in administrative decision making is perhaps clearer and more familiar in the context of environmental regulation than in any other policy area. A large part of the contemporary environmental movement was initiated by an almost "grass-roots" reaction to Rachel Carson's *Silent Spring,* and it has become quite common to hear about citizen groups advancing the environmentalist cause in agency proceedings, in court, and in the media. Contemporary accounts can easily give the impression that no major environmental policy is changed or implemented without the involvement, if not the acquiescence, of several well-organized environmental organizations.

Changes in administrative procedures have provided a wide variety of opportunities for environmentalists to attempt to influence environmental policy. The rights to intervene in agency decision making and to participate in public hearings are only the most obvious avenues of influence; the procedural and substantive requirements of the National Enviromental Policy Act indirectly create opportunities for access through litigation which have been frequently utilized. It is tempting to assume that the procedures were enacted at the behest of citizen groups and then to conclude that they facilitate effective participation. In any case, the complex maze of procedural requirements for citizen participation make American public administration in general quite distinctive and constitute a significant departure from traditional bureaucratic values (Rosenbaum, 1976:355–56).

The purposes of this chapter are to analyze the origins of several important changes in formal administrative procedure which have affected citizen participation and to consider their impact on policy. It will be suggested that many of the formal arrangements and doctrines creating citizen access are only partly the result of a desire to enact democratic procedures and expand representativeness. A full understanding of their effectiveness and their unintended consequences requires that the several forces leading to them be appreciated.

ORIGINS OF "CITIZEN PARTICIPATION" PROCEDURES

Although some of the important avenues for citizen participation in administration were instituted during the 1960s and 1970s (for example, intervention in licensing hearings, broadened standing to sue administrators), the basic tools of participation were set in place long before public advocacy was widespread. The Administrative Procedure Act (APA) of 1946 expanded and brought uniformity to the requirements for public hearings prior to administrative rule making, but most agencies were required by their own enabling statutes to hold such hearings even before then. The Federal Register Act made available official documents relating to agency rule making, proposed rule making, and other formal actions a decade earlier. And, perhaps most important of all to modern citizen participation, judicial review of agency action was firmly established and available long before the APA (Jaffe, 1965).

Clearly, governmental procedures and processes were shaped so as to facilitate "external" participation and influence as a result of circumstances or forces that pre-dated the environmental and citizen movements of the 1960s. Three complementary explanations may be offered, none of which indicates a concern for "democratizing" administrative decisions: (1) a conservative legal movement to constrain official administrative regulatory authority, (2) a legislative concern with controlling the aggressiveness of regulatory agencies with delegated legislative power, and (3) a generalized administrative interest in developing and maintaining independent political power bases.

The Legal-Conservative Coalition and Administrative Procedure

A strict constructionist interpretation of the Constitution suggests that administrative power itself is inherently illegitimate, not only because it is not directly provided for by the Constitution but because Article 1, Section 1 states: "All legislative Powers herein granted shall be vested in a Congress of the United States." Hence, such powers cannot be delegated to administrators. This idea was seized upon by traditional legal thinkers who were motivated by a concern for fundamental constitutional values and by those who wanted to reduce the growth in public control of private enterprise (Ethridge, 1979, ch. 1). Much to the dismay of legal conservatives who, like Roscoe Pound, were increasingly alarmed at the rise of "administrative absolutism" (Verkuil, 1984:13), the Supreme Court upheld the constitutionality of virtually all delegations of administrative power (Robinson, Gellhorn, Bruff, 1980, ch. 2). The notable exceptions in 1935 have been largely insignificant in the subsequent development of constitutional law (Davis, 1975, ch. 2).

Reform of administrative procedure became the next objective of those who had wanted to limit the power of government regulation by denying delegation itself. If businesses were to be subjected to administrative authority, agencies should at least be forced to exercise that authority through procedures that provided legal protections and rights similar to those which characterized judicial proceedings. The "judicialization" of the administrative process was most extensively mandated by the 1939 Walter-Logan Bill, passed by Congress but vetoed by

President Franklin D. Roosevelt. It is interesting to note how far this bill would have gone in creating opportunities for participation in agency decision making. For example, literally any person "aggrieved" by an administrative decision could demand a trial-type hearing, and the propriety of existing rules and regulations could be subjected to hearings if an "interested" party requested it (Verkuil, 1984:15). Moreover, judicial review was to be available at the request of any interested person, effectively granting standing to all citizens to sue administrative agencies.

The more moderate and flexible Administrative Procedure Act of 1946 was responsive to the demands of public administrationists, the executive branch, academics, and even some legal analysts who saw the need for less rigid administrative procedures. Most important, the APA provided for "informal" rule making (public notice and usually a hearing required, but no trial-type adversary proceedings). Much of the basic framework for citizen access was established in this act.

Even the more recent Freedom of Information Act (FOIA) (actually an amendment to the APA) was not primarily inspired by a concern for "grass-roots" involvement in administration but for legal access to the precedents and records of much information agency action (Schick, 1972; Davis, 1975, ch. 20). The exemptions contained in the FOIA have stirred much controversy in legal circles, since agencies can apparently find many ways to prevent disclosure of certain items of information. From a more political viewpoint, it is clear that the provisions have been important selectively to groups with significant legal expertise.

Taken together, many aspects of administrative procedure used by environmentalist groups were, ironically perhaps, designed for very different purposes. In this connection, it is interesting that a major public administration textbook published in 1950 predicted that the then new procedural reforms of the APA would probably facilitate participation by regulated groups and others with an interest in slowing or moderating government regulation (Simon, Smithburg, Thompson, 1950:521). The legal origins of many reformed procedures would probably surprise many contemporary citizen and environmental activists.

Legislative Motivations and Administrative Procedure

During recent years, several analysts have constructed theories of legislative behavior which emphasize the legislator's political self-interest as a factor determining legislative oversight, bill passage, casework activities, and other behavior (Niskanen, 1975; Fiorina, 1981; Aranson et al., 1982). Ideology and internal organizational norms and processes also influence behavior, but contemporary inquiry has produced some intriguing results by evaluating the impact of self-interest. In this connection, it is highly probable that some important changes relevant to administrative procedure which produce access opportunities for environmentalist or other citizen groups had their origin in legislator self-interest.

The essential idea here is rather simple: legislators delegate decision-making authority to administrators (largely) because they want to avoid the political and other costs of making the decisions themselves, but they include in their delegations procedural restrictions and limits on the scope of agency power so that the administrators can be prevented from making decisions against legislative preferences. Thus, a system of agencies with significant legal powers but guided and confined by elaborate procedural requirements can be seen as the result of legislators rationally pursuing their political advantage (Noll, Peck, McGowan, 1974; Ethridge, 1984; McCubbins, 1985).

That legislators delegate to "shift the responsibility" for controversial regulatory policy is perhaps clearer than the idea that they institute procedural requirements to guide agency action. Delegation allows a legislator to distance himself or herself from regulatory actions, allowing more flexibility in political posturing since the legislator does not have to proclaim agreement or disagreement with a specific regulatory action. This motivation is, of course, supplemented by the more obvious pressures to delegate—limits on time, staff resources, and technical understanding of regulatory details.

McCubbins recently suggested that this line of thought apparently assumes that "delegation does not change the actual policy adopted, and that the agency chooses precisely the regulatory policy Congress wants" (1985:723). Clearly, agencies may make choices which are seriously at odds with legislative preferences. Administrators may be ideologically committed to a maverick alternative, they may be influenced by interest groups, or they may develop and make choices on which legislators had no clear preferences when the delegated authority was granted. In all of these and many other circumstances, a situation can develop in which agencies with delegated power may take actions inconsistent with legislative wishes.

Thus, legislators find themselves in a dilemma. They want to avoid direct action to minimize political costs but they are not always willing to allow others (administrators) to make decisions because the outcomes may not be to their liking. It is in a legislator's interest to be able both to avoid making some decisions *and* to limit the latitude of the actual decision makers. One way to accomplish this is to continue delegation while establishing procedural requirements which influence agency decisions. Such requirements may specify "the process of hearings, . . . the points of access for outside parties, the opportunities for judicial review, and standards for review" (McCubbins, 1985:727). Hearing and judicial review requirements, among other effects, make it likely that administrators will be under the same (or similar) array of influences that guide legislators preferences when the actual policy choices are refined and implemented by agency action.

This idea applies most clearly to the legislative veto procedure adopted in many states and applied broadly in Congress until recently held unconstitutional (in *Immigration and Naturalization Service v. Chadha*, 77 L. Ed. 2d 317). The ability to veto a troublesome agency action became more attractive when legislatures were delegating power to agencies in increasingly controversial policy arenas during the 1960s and 1970s. The growth of veto machinery can be seen as a way to continue delegation while maintaining the option to "put out fires" started by errant agency choices (Ethridge, 1984).

Special characteristics of environmental regulation may make these legislator motivations particularly important. McCubbins argued that environmental policy is more conflictual and produces more uncertainty of outcomes than, for example, most economic regulation. As a result, legislators should be expected to delegate a relatively broad scope of power to environmenal regulators (because of the conflict) *and* to require more elaborate administrative procedures (to control the uncertainty) (McCubbins, 1985:745).

Thus, legislator self-interest can be seen as contributing to the procedural framework of contemporary administrative processes. Ironically, it may be the conflict and uncertainty created by the effectiveness of public advocates and other citizens' groups which have led to the procedural changes. The hearings, reviews, and other requirements are arguably designed to allow "corrections" when agencies make decisions which are "overly" responsive to citizen influences.

Administrative Power and Administrative Procedure

Reforms which open administrative agencies to outside influences may be a two-edged sword in terms of legislative-administrative relations. They can limit discretion (as the previous section suggests), but they may also provide a foundation for some measure of administrative independence. Nearly forty years ago, Norton Long argued that "the lifeblood of administration is power" but that the American political system "does not generate enough power at any focal point of leadership" to allow agencies to do their jobs (1949:258). Hence, the administrators must often develop their own power bases. Public hearings and regular consultation with private parties, both those regulated and others, can help to create effective linkages that can be useful in securing budget increases and other benefits. Elaborate procedures may sometimes be actively established by regulatory agencies anxious for their own power positions.

In this connection, it is noteworthy that agencies often do go beyond minimum procedural requirements when citizen participation is involved. State environmental agencies, in particular, often publish notices of their hearings more widely and with a longer lead time than is normally required (Ethridge, 1979). Decisions made after highly visible public consultation can carry greater weight and legitimacy, both in legislative circles and in terms of the agency's public perception, than decisions in which there is little public involvement. Whether or not the procedures lead to participation that actually changes decisions is another matter; the *process* contributes to the power base.

Taken together, legal traditions and legislator and administrator self-interest provide compelling explanations for much of the procedural complexity that characterizes contemporary administration. This is not to say that a generalized belief in democratic values or disinterested support for constitutional principles have been irrelevant, of course. Elaborate judicialized procedures could not have been adopted if they were contrary to widespread American political attitudes. Quite simply, it is argued here that the essential consistency between these values and the *form* and *appearance* of the administrative procedures in question made it possible for the forces discussed above to produce them. The consequences of procedural complexity and "openness" for environmental policy making are addressed in the next section.

ADMINISTRATIVE PROCEDURES, CITIZEN ACCESS, AND ENVIRONMENTAL POLICY

Measuring the effectiveness of changes in administrative procedure is enormously difficult, primarily because of the large number of factors that could be responsible for any effects observed in policy or behavior. Nonetheless, several analysts have studied the problem, using a variety of methods and approaches. Two conclusions are frequently encountered: (1) elaborate administrative procedures have had little success in "democratizing" administrative decision making, and (2) the access that is produced is systematically unrepresentative of the public interest.

It is not difficult, of course, to conclude that citizen participation procedures have "failed" to democratize the administrative process when one evaluates actual experiences in terms of the far-fetched hopes or claims of the most outspoken adherents of procedural reform. The Administrative Procedure Act's requirements for public involvement in agency rule making have been called, for example, an approximation of "participatory democracy" (Bonfield, 1975). Even a casual observer can easily note the empty or near-empty hearing rooms and the frequently pointless interchanges that occur during agency rule-making hearings. Even those with large numbers of participants often become meaningless displays of ideological fervor that have no impact on policy or implementation (Ethridge, 1980). That these circumstances do not approximate "participatory democracy" is both obvious and trivial.

Evaluations made from a more reasonable footing produce mixed results at best. Walter Rosenbaum (1976) reported on several agencies' experiences with the citizen participation requirements that were becoming more elaborate during the 1960s. According to Rosenbaum, the programs were generally failures (1976:356). Results were disappointing for several reasons, including lax enforcement of some procedures, but the most striking conclusion had to do with the narrow range of participants interested in the access opportunities. Even in the area of environmental regulation, citizen participation fell short of most expectations; despite a vigorous Environmental Protection Agency (EPA) effort, that agency's "Water Quality Workshops" failed to generate more than negligible representation from a broad range of interests. Moreover, "eight of every ten participants were likely to be government officials or consultants to government bodies" (Rosenbaum, 1976:374).

A quantitative study of the relationship between the "openness" of state administrative procedures and the "aggressiveness" of state environmental regulations was generally consistent with Rosenbaum's observations (Ethridge, 1982). It was found that "states with generally reformed procedures . . . tend to have more stringent emission standards" for sulfur dioxide emissions (499). The correlations were quite small, however. Interestingly, they were higher for states which had small environmental lobbies; that is, procedural reform was most strongly associated with the strictness of emission standards in states in which the environmental lobbies were smaller (Ethridge, 1982:503).

Two points about these results should be emphasized here. First, they say nothing about actual citizen participation behavior. The correlations were between the "openness" indicated by the state statutes and the strictness of the pollution standards. Thus, it is very difficult to see direct support in these findings for any causal hypothesis, since both the stricter standards and the more "reformed" procedures could be caused by some factor not included in the research. Second, the weakness of the results means that many states with elaborate procedures had relatively lax pollution standards and some states with unreformed procedures had stringent standards. The availability of procedures for participation did not produce a fundamental, widespread change in policy.

Perhaps more important than the failure to produce substantial public participation are the representational shortcomings of the access opportunities that the procedures do produce. Rosenbaum reported that most participants he observed "end toward the well-educated, affluent middle- to upper-class individuals" (1976:372). Similarly, Cupps noted that many spokespersons for the environment are often pursuing "middle and upper class concerns which are addressed for the most part at the expense of the poor, the aged, and urban and ethnic minorities" (1977:481).

It should not be surprising, therefore, that the citizen participation encouraged by formal hearing procedures has not often contributed to the "complicated, creative balancing of conflicting interests in controversial areas" (Cupps, 1977:481). Instead, it has frequently served to make discussions of public policies more ideological, more difficult, and less representative of broader public interests.

A special procedure of interest in environmental policy is the requirement for environmental impact statements contained in the National Environmental Policy Act (NEPA) of 1969. While not normally considered a procedure for facilitating public participation, the EIS requirement has created numerous litigation opportunities, effectively used by environmental groups in particular. Three recent court cases provide a good basis for evaluating the policy impact of the citizen access produced by this procedure.

From the perspective of an environmental activist, the EIS requirement was doubtlessly seen as a major reform. Public officials would presumably be forced to study and reassess objectively projects with significant environmental impacts, and this would surely mean that fewer harmful projects would be approved. Judicial interpretation of this procedure provides some interesting insights into the efficacy of procedural change as a vehicle for policy change.

Section 102(2)(c) of the National Environmental Policy Act of 1969 (42 U.S.C.A. 4331 et seq.) states that the Environmental Impact Statement (EIS) required before any "proposal for legislation" or any "major federal action" that "significantly affects the quality of the human environment" include the following:

(i) the environmental impact of the proposed action;

(ii) any adverse environmental effects which cannot be avoided should the proposal be implemented;

(iii) alternatives to the proposed action;

(iv) the relationship between local short term uses of man's environment and the maintenance and enhancement of long-term productivity;

(v) any irreversible and irretrievable commitments of resources which would be involved in the proposed action should it be implemented.

Environmentalist-oriented citizen groups have used the requirement as a legal foundation for lawsuits when agencies are involved in projects which allegedly degrade the environment. One of the most important legal issues raised had to do with the objectivity of the EIS produced—can the law have been adequately followed if the EIS was written by someone "committed" to the project in question? *Environmental Defense Fund, Inc. v. Corps of Engineers (EDF)*, 470 U.S. 289, 1973, addressed this concern. The facts provide an excellent context for evaluating the limits of the EIS procedural requirements.

The *EDF* case had to do with the Gillham Dam project on the Cossatot River in Arkansas. The project was initiated in 1963, long before the EIS requirement was enacted. By the time NEPA was passed, two-thirds of the project had been completed, at a cost of some $10 million. The EIS, of course, had to be submitted before the dam could be completed (it would entail the flooding of 1,370 acres of wilderness), and the Corps of Engineers did so, producing a 1,700-page document at a cost of a quarter of a million dollars.

The environmental group claimed that the substance of the EIS was insufficient in its discussion of alternatives and in its disclosure of environmental harms, but the most important claim had to do with the position and attitude of the official primarily responsible for the document. The Corps assigned one of its District Engineers to direct the preparation of the EIS, an official who had, in a local Chamber of Commerce meeting, discussed the advantages of the forthcoming dam and the fact that it would surely be completed. According to the Environmental Defense Fund, it could not have been the intention of Congress to allow an EIS to be written by someone who had already decided (and publicly proclaimed) that the project in question should go forward.

The Court of Appeals concluded that while NEPA requires agencies to "objectively evaluate their projects," it does not require agency officials to be "subjectively impartial." The law only requires "good faith objectivity" and that agencies "consider and give effect to the environmental goals set forth in the Act." Although a court could properly inquire into the merits of the agency's decision regarding an environmentally relevant project, and although that review could properly include an analysis of the substantive completeness and soundness of the EIS, judicial inquiry would ultimately focus upon whether or not the agency's decision was "arbitrary and capricious." The Gillham Dam project was acceptable in this sense.

Consequently, the procedural requirement contained in NEPA, although producing greater public awareness of agency projects and providing an opportunity to evaluate agency decisions on environmental impact assessment, did not transfer administrative discretion from agencies to the public. Citizen groups could see NEPA to demand that agencies be "reasonable" but not to outlaw decisions with adverse environmental impacts.

The timing of the required EIS was at issue in *Kleppe v. Sierra Club*, 426 U.S. 390, 1976. Essentially, the Sierra Club claimed that the Interior Department should be required to produce an

EIS for an apparently projected regional development of coal reserves in an area identified as the "Northern Great Plains." EISs had been required for particular coal lease plans within the region, but not for the region as a whole. The Supreme Court flatly concluded that NEPA only requires an EIS for "proposals for major federal actions" and that, since no such action had been proposed at the regional level, no EIS was required. The Court noted that requiring EISs when projects were being "conceived" or "imagined" would "leave agencies uncertain as to their procedural duties." The Sierra Club, quite reasonably perhaps, argued that by the time a formal proposal is made, the EIS could be nothing more than a post hoc rationalization of a decision already set in place. Nonetheless, the procedural requirement would not be more broadly applied.

Vermont Yankee Nuclear Power Corp. v. Natural Resources Defense Council, Inc., 435 U.S. 519, 1978, is one of the most important and most controversial administrative law cases of recent decades. A small part of the dispute had to do with the NEPA procedural requirement. NRDC and other environmental groups asserted that in the EIS for the power plant, alternatives to the project were not adequately represented. In particular, the statement made no mention of "energy conservation" as an alternative to building a nuclear power plant. If the Court had agreed with the environmentalists, any EIS could be held invalid (and the project in question disapproved or delayed) whenever a plaintiff with standing to sue could conceive of an alternative not discussed in the EIS. The Court concluded that such a situation was not intended by Congress and that the Vermont Yankee EIS was acceptable. As Justice William Rehnquist stated in the unanimous opinion:

Nuclear energy may some day be a cheap, safe source of energy or it may not. But Congress has made a choice to at least try nuclear energy. . . . Time may prove wrong the decision to develop nuclear energy, but it is Congress or the States within their appropriate agencies which must eventually make that judgment.

Thus, NEPA would not be construed as giving litigants the power to second-guess policy judgments—it only would allow

them to police agencies' reasonableness in exposing themselves
to questions of environmental impact. The actual project decisions would not be changed by NEPA's procedural requirements or by the spirit of environmental values that motivated
its enactment.

THE DEMOCRATIC EFFICACY OF
ADMINISTRATIVE PROCEDURE

Lynton Caldwell (1975) once noted that the American political system does not often facilitate affective policy making in
the area of environmental protection, essentially because the
"environment" as a concept requires comprehensive, long-range
analysis and conceptualization, neither of which is encouraged
by the fragmented, particularistic representation of interests so
much a part of American politics. Instead of addressing the
environment appropriately, the problem is commonly defined
as a "pollution control" problem, limiting our ability to deal
with the multifaceted, complex, interrelated issues of the environment in an effective way.

Citizen participation and the procedures designed to encourage and accommodate it have been viewed by some as a way
to make public policy genuinely responsive to the broadly based
needs and demands which comprise the public interest (Marini, 1971). In no policy area has this idea been more discussed
than in the case of environmental protection. However, a considerable body of experience with procedural changes, included both those which are intended simply to "open" public
agencies and the more specific NEPA requirements, suggests
that procedural change will not likely produce such a fundamental improvement in responsiveness. The system's tendency
to address environmental issues incompletely, in Caldwell's
sense, will not be corrected by procedural requirements.

Appreciating the historical origins of the procedural foundations for citizen access to agency decision making is helpful in
understanding why they have not produced a hoped-for shift
in the direction of broader democratization of administration.
Perhaps most important, procedures designed under the influence of legal values and doctrines are clearly better suited to

producing effective adversarial arrangements with appropriate protections of private rights than to creating avenues for public involvement in policy making. The APA and other procedural requirements are certainly relevant to citizen access, but we should probably not be surprised that they create little effective public influence; the legal containment of administrative discretion does not necessarily generate a stronger public direction of agencies. Perhaps safeguarding private rights and advocating representativeness share a common rhetoric at some level of abstraction, but the legal doctrines which produce the former are not broadly democratizing.

Similarly, legislative and administrative motivations can be seen as contributing to procedural requirements in order to improve and maintain political advantage. That such requirements fail to create genuine public influence should hardly be remarkable. Instead, they enable both legislators and agencies to respond to the same influences that guide their preferences and behavior in general. Patterns of political responsibility are not easily changed.

In light of the failure of procedural reform to generate broadened public involvement, it is often troubling to consider what is happening to the policy process. Rosenbaum expresses the concerns succinctly:

The new participation may actually be creating a new influence structure which selective interests, already administratively active, have exploited in hope of greater success; one might well expect the agency-group relationship to stabilize within the structure over time without necessarily producing any strong pressures for greater heterogeneity of representation. (1976:374)

Truly public representation, or even representation of a broader array of selective interests, has not been produced effectively or consistently by procedural changes. In terms of "'democratic administration,'" the system may not be any better than it was several decades ago.

An analysis of bureaucracy, representation, and administrative procedure suggests, above all, that democratic decision making depends upon effective mobilization of the "public interest." Simply providing access points will not suffice if the broad-based mobilization is absent. The procedural opportunities instead create somewhat better access for interests already influential. In the case of environmental policy especially, this appears to be the soundest conclusion.

REFERENCES

Aranson, Peter, Ernest Gellhorn, and Glen Robinson 1982
        "A Theory of Legislative Delegation," *Cornell Law Review* 68:1–67.
Bonfield, Arthur E. 1975
        "The Iowa Administrative Procedure Act," *Iowa Law Review* 60:731–936.
Caldwell, Lynton, C. 1975
        "Responsiveness and Responsibility: The Anomalous Problem of the Environment," in Leroy Rieselbach, ed., *People vs. Government: The Representativeness of American Institutions*. (Bloomington: Indiana University Press).
Cupps, D. Stephen 1977
        "Emerging Problems of Citizen Participation," *Public Administration Review* 37:478–87.
Davis, Kenneth C. 1975
        Administrative Law and Government, 2d ed. (St. Paul, Minn.: West Publishing).
Ethridge, Marcus E. 1979
        "The Effect of Administrative Procedure on Environmental Policy Implementation: A Comparative State Study." Ph.D. dissertation, Vanderbilt University, Nashville, Tenn.
——— 1980
        "Agency Responses to Citizen Participation Requirements: An Analysis of the Tennessee Experience," *Midwest Review of Public Administration* 14:95–104.
——— 1982
        "The Policy Impact of Citizen Participation Requirements: A Comparative State Study," *American Politics Quarterly* 10:489–509.
——— 1984
        "A Political-Institutional Interpretation of Legislative Oversight Mechanisms and Behavior," *Policy* 17:340–59.
Fiorina, Morris, 1981
        "Congressional Control of the Bureaucracy: A Mismatch of In-

centives and Capabilities," in Lawrence Dodd and Bruce Oppenheimer, eds., *Congress Reconsidered*, 2d Ed. (Washington, D.C.: Congressional Quarterly Press).

Jaffe, Louis L. 1965
Judicial Control of Administrative Action. (Boston: Little, Brown).

Long, Norton 1949
"Power and Administration," *Public Administration Review* 9:257–64.

McCubbins, Matthew D. 1985
"The Legislative Design of Regulatory Structure," *American Journal of Political Science* 29:721–48.

Marini, Frank, ed. 1971
Toward a New Public Administration. (New York: Chandler Publishing Co.).

Niskanen, William 1975
"Bureaucrats and Politicians," *Journal of Law and Economics* 18:617–43.

Noll, Roger, M. J. Peck, and J. J. McGowan 1974
Economic Aspects of Television Regulation. (Washington, D.C.: Brookings Institution).

Robinson, Glen O., Ernest Gellhorn, and Harold Bruff.
The Administrative Process, 2d ed. (St. Paul, Minn.: West Publishing).

Rosenbaum, Walter A. 1976
"The Paradoxes of Public Participation," *Administration and Society* 8:3:355–83.

Schick, Allan 1972
"Let the Sunshine In," *The Bureaucrat* 1:2:156–60.

Simon, Herbert, Donald Smithburg, and Victor Thompson 1950
Public Administration. (New York: Knopf).

Verkuil, Paul A. 1984
"The Emerging Concept of Administrative Procedure," in Howard Ball, ed., *Federal Administrative Agencies*. (Englewood Cliffs, N.J.: Prentice-Hall).

7

Consumers and Health Planning: Mobilization of Bias?

JACK DESARIO

During the 1960s, major battles were waged to win citizens the right to participate in public planning and administration. In the 1970s, consumer involvement in public agencies became widely accepted as one of the "most distinctive features of American administration" (Cupps, 1977:478). Early citizen participation legislation, as represented by maximum feasible participation clauses, was considered to be too vague conceptually and procedurally. Federal legislation within the last decade has, it is believed, vigorously advanced the consumer participation cause through the more precise definition of consumers and their role in administration. One of the most prominent examples of this "new generation" of planning was Public Law 93–641: the National Health Planning and Resources Development Act. This law created over 200 areawide planning agencies, known as Health Service Agencies (HSAs), which were expected to plan for all aspects of their health service areas. Health planning decisions within HSAs have been entrusted to a governing board. These boards were required, by law, to include a majority of health care consumers. The remainder of the board was to consist of health care providers—physicians, hospital administrators, and so on.

Generally, the inclusion of citizen groups in planning has been received with a great deal of enthusiasm and expectation by many public interest groups. However, the Reagan administration has called for the elimination of federal financial support to many of these innovative planning programs, including HSAs. Despite this action, most states have retained their current health planning structures. The perceived social importance of this process by the states has led them to provide funds for this activity. Given these changing dynamics and assumptions, it is important to evaluate the normative and substantive contributions of legislated consumer participation. The question of the proper role of citizens in the administration of public programs—whether at the federal, state, or local level—will continue to be an issue of great importance and controversy.

The merits of citizen participation have been debated by many authors, and this analysis will attempt to provide more information about the perceptions, characteristics, and contributions of this group of participants. It must be determined whether these newly enfranchised groups are imperfectly mobilized, if they provide our society with a "representative" and "accountable" administration process, and if they are working on behalf of the "public welfare."

Some social commentators now question whether citizen groups effectively reflect the viewpoints of their constituencies. D. Stephen Cupps (1977:481) summarizes the beliefs of this growing body of thought when he writes that these "self-appointed spokesmen for the public are often speaking for a much smaller segment of the public than they are to admit. . . . [C]onsumer, environmental, and other so-called 'public interest' issues are in reality middle and upper middle class concerns which are addressed for the most part at the expense of the poor, the aged, and urban and ethnic minorities." In other words, "responsible people and representatives do not always go together" (Bireland, 1971:293).

Any analysis of these issues must first begin with a consideration of the conceptual and operational dimensions of the term "representation." The belief in "representativeness" is central to the origins and implementation of many issues related to citizen participation. Unfortunately, most of the common and simplistic conceptions of representation have become obsolete as the scale of "mass society renders inoperable the decision mechanisms of classical democracy" (Fagence, 1977:52). The evolving complexities and dilemmas of representativeness which have come about have not been adequately considered and defined by government officials. This conceptual void can only make a substantial contribution to current organization difficulties.

In modern societies, representativeness as a goal or process is not "achieved through any single channel" (Pennock, 1968:27). Instead, as James Pennock observes, there exists "numerous and varied avenues of representation, each by virtue of its own peculiar nature, seeing, reflecting, attempting to effectuate a slightly different facet of that great conglomerate of desires and interests that make up the electorate" (1968:27). Based upon the writings of a diversity of authors, four main senses of representation emerge: descriptive, substantive, ascriptive, and formal political representation (Pitkin, 1967; Eulaud and Prewitt, 1973; Griffiths, 1960). Descriptive representation refers to the theory that people are incorporated into a decision-making body because they reflect the characteristics of a larger group, the assumption being that similar characteristics will insure the promotion of common interests. Substantive representation maintains that individuals should be selected to participate in a process not because they share common characteristics but because they display a commitment to and interest in a policy perspective and tend to represent a group by working for and espousing these interests. Ascriptive forms of representation refer to the process whereby population groups completely delegate decision-making authority to particular individuals because the clientele lack the superior or specialized knowledge required by the situation (lawyers, for example). The last type of representation—formal political—refers to political officeholders who are entrusted with decision-making power which they can exercise in the manner they deem most appropriate.

In the present context of direct citizen participation in public bureaucracies, descriptive and substantive representativeness assume the greatest importance to decision making. Congress, while neglecting to review the structural implications of these representational forms, has advised health systems agencies to promote both of these schemes (Chesney, 1978:5). A careful examination of the intrinsic qualities of descriptive and substantive representation and the political participation literature suggests that each of these representational schemes may have a differential impact upon the related and fundamental issues of accountability, responsiveness, competence, and the consolidation of power. We will now investigate how successfully these forms of citizen participation are being advanced and their operational contributions.

The opportunity for direct participation by citizen groups was greatly enhanced by health planning legislation. According to the Health Planning and Resources Development Act, which still provides the framework for current health planning structures, health systems agencies must have consumer majorities on their governing boards which are "broadly representative of the social, economic, linguistic, and racial populations" of their areas (U.S. Congress, 1975). Utilizing the New York–Pennsylvania (NY–Penn) HSA as an example, we will determine the extent to which these health planning agencies can and do represent the concerns and characteristics of their areas. The NY-Penn HSA governing body has 137 members of which 70 are consumers (51 percent) and 67 are providers (49 percent) of health care. This clear consumer majority is not, however, demographically representative of the community. Table 7.1 and 7.2 demonstrate that while parity rates for consumer members of the board are much more equitable in all cases, as compared to the total membership, many citizen groups are severely underrepresented. Blacks in the NY-Penn HSA are overrepresented proportionately on the governing board, while women are underrepresented. Regardless of sex or ethnic group, consumer members on the governing board tend to be disproportionately from the upper social class. Over 34 percent of the consumer members on the board have a personal income exceeding $25,000, in comparison to only 15 percent for the general community. Although 36 percent of the general population has an income under $10,000, only 19 percent of the consumer board members are from this low-income category.

The disproportionate number of consumers from high socioeconomic groups versus middle- or low-status groups is further

Table 7.1
Parity Rates for Selected Demographic Characteristics of Governing Board and for Consumer Members on Board

Group	Governing Board	Consumer Members on Board
Blacks	180%	285%
Women	67%	84%
Income Groups		
Under $10,000	33%	53%
$10,000-14,999	45%	64%
$15,000-24,999	96%	122%
$25,000 and over	294%	227%

The very small percentage of blacks in the general community (2%) helps to account for these large percentages.
Source: Community figures are based upon the 1979–80 population estimates collected by the *Marketing Economics Guide*.
Board percentages were provided by the NY-Penn HSA based upon a complete enumeration of their numbers.

Note: Parity Rate $= \dfrac{\% \text{ of group on board}}{\% \text{ of group in community}}$

Table 7.2
Comparison of Income Levels for Community, Governing Board, and Consumers on Governing Board

Income	Community	Governing Board	Consumers on Governing Board
Under $10,000	36%	12%	19%
$10,000-14,999	22%	10%	14%
$15,000-24,999	27%	26%	33%
$25,000 and over	15%	52%	34%
	100%	100%	100%

confined when educational and occupational backgrounds are displayed. Tables 7.3 and 7.4, derived from questionnaires administered to the governing board and a random sample of the community, indicate that the great majority of the board membership, including consumer members of the board, belong to the highest occupational and educational groups. Although consumer members are slightly less concentrated in these high-status categories than the total membership, they are far from representative (demographically) of the population of the area. Fifty percent of the consumers on the board have at least some advanced graduate training, compared to only 7 percent of the community. Eighty-three percent of these consumers are professional, technical, or managerial workers versus 41 percent of the community. Blue-collar professions such as laborers, operatives, and craftsmen are not represented among consumer members, even though they account for 35 percent of the workforce in the region.

The NY–Penn HSA has obviously not been able to implement successfully the conception of descriptive or demographic representation. This failure must not, however, be considered

Table 7.3
Comparison of Educational Levels of Community with Educational Levels of the Governing Board and Consumer Members on the Governing Board

Education	Community	Governing Board	Consumers on Governing Board
12 years or less	63%	11%*	18%*
Some college or college graduate	30%	24%	32%
Graduate training	7%	65%*	50%*
	100%	100%	100%
	N= 411	N= 105	N= 56

*Indicates figure from which the community survey differs at a significance level of greater than 99%.

Source: Information for this table was derived from the administration of questionnaires to the community and the governing board.

Note: Computational formula for Z-values to determine the statistical significance between proportions is as follows:

$$Ps - Pu = Z\frac{\sqrt{P \cdot Q}}{\sqrt{N}}$$

Table 7.4

Comparison of Community Occupations with Occupations of Governing Board and Consumer Members on the Governing Board

Occupation	Community	Governing Board	Consumers on Governing Board
Professional and Technical	25%	64%*	57%*
Managerial and Administrative	16%	25%*	26%*
Clerical and Sales	17%	8%*	10%*
Craftsmen	11%	0%*	0%*
Operatives	13%	0%*	0%*
Service Workers	7%	3%	7%
Farm and Non-Farm Laborers	11%	0%*	0%*
	100%	100%	100%
	N= 411	N= 105	N = 56

*Indicates figure from which the community survey differs at a significance level of greater than 99%.

Source: Information for this table was derived from the administration of questionnaires to the community and the governing board.

symptomatic of only this particular agency. Statistics collected by the Department of Health, Education, and Welfare for 134 governing boards indicate that on the average over 86 percent of all working consumer members are classified as being in professional and/or managerial positions (Chesney, 1978:10). This percentage, while exceeding NY–Penn's, closely parallels the same general employment pattern of consumer board members. Findings such as these, despite explicit directives to promote equality, reaffirm the general upper-class slant of consumer groups in planning and administration and heighten the theoretical and practical importance of the following exposition of the causes and impact of this demographic bias. The implications of a "professional consumer model" of citizen participation for our society must be studied in detail.

An important conceptual link related to these issues which will be probed is the question of whether it is possible to achieve "substantive representation" despite our inability to approximate "descriptive representation." Answers to this representational dilemma will be provided by a review of the attitudinal responses of community and planning groups. This reconstruction and comparison of health care values was greatly facilitated by the work of Elaine Riska and James Taylor (1978), who devised attitudinal scales which assess an individual's approach to health and the role of government. Two major viewpoints underline the scale. On the one hand is the "libertarian" who stresses the virtues of the free market and individual freedom, and on the other is the "egalitarian" who believes in a positive or welfare state which secures social rights. This indicator is of particular importance to this study and has been included because it reveals the outlook of planning groups that are ultimately responsible for the development of a public health planning strategy which must take a stand on this issue. It is assumed that one's attitudes are related to the particular course of action one will select and advocate.

Table 7.5 presents a comparison of board member and community opinions in regard to five questions related to the proper role of government in the health care field. In four of the five questions, the general population's view is significantly different (at a confidence level of at least 95 percent) from that of the

governing board. The board as a whole tends to be less favor-
ably disposed toward government intervention in the health
care economy, government placement of physicians, and national health insurance. Somewhat of a surprise, in light of these
attitudes, is the finding that the governing board is very supportive of government review of hospital purchases (Certificate
of Need [CON]).

The board's endorsement of CON can be interpreted in two
ways. Some health analysts suggest that CON may be viewed
by providers as a method of institutionalizing the dominance
and importance of existing hospitals in an effort to insure their
market share. Another interpretation of the overwhelming acceptance of the contributions of CON can be attributed to the
fact that the main responsibilities for implementing this process
have been delegated to HSAs and the members of their governing boards. This situation may indicate that familiarity with
a process eases it of many of its ominous connotations—involvement breeds legitimacy.

The remaining attitudes are much more consistent with what
one might expect fromm a planning board that has a large
provider contingent. Governing board members as a group are
not as enthusiastic about the rewards of national health insurance, government placement of physicians, and government
intervention into the economy. For example, while 60 percent
of the community favors the institution of some form of national health insurance, only 49 percent of the board feels the
same way. A large part of the difference between these groups
can be attributed to the fact that only 38 percent of the providers agree with the need for national health insurance. Providers also play a major role in explaining attitudinal differences
between the governing board and the community in regard to
the role of the government in the health care market. Forty-five
percent of the general population believes that government can
prevent higher costs, while 35 percent of the board concurs.
When we consider that only 20 percent of the providers favor
government intervention to control health costs, it is apparent
that this group accounts for almost all of the differences in perceptions between the board and the community for this issue.

A comparison of the values of consumer members of the board

Table 7.5

Comparison of Community, Governing Board, and Consumer Members on Governing Board Attitudes Toward Government Intervention in the Health Care Field

Government Intervention Questions	Community	Governing Board	Consumers On Governing Board
Government intervention can prevent higher costs--% strongly or somewhat agree	44.8	33.3*	44.6
Private market is the basic strength of health care--% strongly or somewhat agree	33.3	35.2	44.6*
Government should place physicians in needy areas--% strongly or somewhat agree	54.2	49.5**	53.6
Government should review expensive hospital purchases--% strongly or somewhat agree	59.8	80.9*	89.3*
Government should institute some form of National Health Insurance--% strongly or somewhat agree	60.3	48.6*	57.1
	N= 411	N= 105	N= 55

*Indicates figure from which community survey differs at a significance level greater than 99%.

**Indicates figure from which community survey differs at a significance level of about 95%.

Source: Information derived for this table was derived from the administration of questionnaires to the community and the governing board.

with those of the community reveals that this "professional consumer" group, although it is not "demographically representative," does seem to convey general community attitudes more accurately than the governing board as a whole. While the view of the board reflects that of the community for only one issue, these consumers articulate the prevailing sentiment for three of the five responses. Consumer opinions toward national health insurance, government placement of physicians, and government intervention in the health care market display no statistically significant difference from those of the community. However, an analysis of the influence of the social class of consumers in respect to their attitudes toward government intervention does distinguish some important variations among consumers. For the four issues examined (CON was excluded due to the abnormally high amount of agreement and the unusual circumstances which surround it), there is a strong relationship between socio-economic status (SES) and the consumer attitudes. It was found that for most of the issues reviewed, as the SES category of the respondents increased, they were as a group less inclined to favor government activities. Conversely, low-status groups expressed very favorable opinions of government initiatives. Table 7.6, utilizing income data, best illustrates the strength of this relationship between SES and attitudes toward government intervention for these four issues (analyses of educational and occupational backgrounds produced similar results). Low-income groups, in most cases, are twice as likely as the high economic group to favor government involvement in health care—programs such as placement of physicians, cost control, and national health insurance.

The explanation for this divergent pattern is probably rooted within the social, economic, and cultural conditions that are dictated by an individual's SES. Most low-income individuals cannot afford the financial burdens imposed by medical hardship (they lack disposable income and comprehensive insurance policies which are provided to workers in more prestigious occupations), and they tend to reside in rural and urban areas which are economically and medically depressed. In summary, the urgent need for medical aid of all kinds is a sa-

Table 7.6

Relationship Between Consumer Attitudes Toward Government Intervention Indicators and Social Class, by Income Categories

Income of Consumer Members

Government Can Prevent Higher Costs	Under $10,000	$10,000-$14,999	$15,000-$24,999	$25,000 and over
Agree	73%	40%	46%	23%
Disagree	18%	60%	42%	69%
Neither	9%	-	4%	8%
Don't know	-	-	8%	-
	N= 11	N= 5	N= 26	N= 13

Government Should Place Physicians in Needy Areas	Under $10,000	$10,000-$14,999	$15,000-$24,999	$25,000 and over
Agree	82%	80%	46%	38%
Disagree	18%	20%	12%	31%
Neither	-	-	38%	31%
Don't know	-	-	4%	-
	N= 11	N= 5	N= 26	N= 13

Income of Consumer Members

Private Market is Basic Strength	Under $10,000	$10,000-$14,999	$15,000-$24,999	$25,000 and over
Agree	45%	40%	46%	38%
Disagree	36%	60%	50%	39%
Neither	18%	-	-	8%
Don't know	-	-	4%	15%
	N= 11	N= 5	N= 26	N= 13

Favor National Health Insurance	Under $10,000	$10,000-$14,999	$15,000-$24,999	$25,000 and over
Agree	82%	40%	54%	54%
Disagree	9%	60%	31%	31%
Neither	9%	-	4%	15%
Don't know	-	-	12%	-
	N= 11	N= 5	N= 26	N= 13

Source: Information from this table was derived from the administration of questionnaires to the governing board.

lient issue for them, which enhances their view of government as a legitimate source of assistance. Robert Alford (1975:254–55) expounds upon the perspectives of consumers from different SES strata when he notes that upper- and middle-class consumers of health care are well served by the dominant characteristics of the health care system, such as fee-for-service physicians and hospitals, as they are now, so these particular consumers have "no incentive to change the system and, in fact, have compelling incentives to keep it the way it is. If there were a move to open up the hospitals and best surgeons to the public on the basis of need rather than on the basis of ability to purchase care, the only possible results would be to reduce their access to the market."

The different social valuations of these SES groups are also reflected in their identification of the most important health care problems of the region. Low-income groups list the need for providing more and better access to physicians and hospitals, curbing the rise in health care costs. Middle- and upper-income groups identified some of these issues, but a larger number identified the establishment of new or bigger programs such as home health care, mental health services, alcohol and drug rehabilitation, and a general desire to promote better coordination as the most important health care priorities. The essential difference between these concerns is that low-status respondents repeatedly expressed the need for basic health care reform and reorganization while middle- and upper-class respondents are more interested in the expansion and integration of health facilities as they now exist and, thus, more limited reform. Both of these sets of demands are important to the health planning process, but as a result of the disproportionate number of high-income groups, there is a mobilization of bias toward the latter perspective. (For a more comprehensive review of the concept of mobilization of bias, see Backrach and Baratz, 1962 and 1963).

The demographic bias of the NY–Penn planning agency should, however, not be viewed as a product of a conspiracy among SES elites seeking to hold and/or maintain a dominant position of power. All members of the governing board are self-selected volunteers, and there simply has been a paucity of applications from low-status individuals. This underrepresentation of low SES groups on planning boards is consistent with political participation studies, conducted throughout the country, which repeatedly document the fact that for all avenues of participation higher socio-economic groups are more likely to possess higher "civic orientation" levels which precipitates higher rates of participation (Verba and Nie, 1972). The upper-class bias of planning boards must therefore be seen "as a logical outgrowth of the American process of political participation which produces representatives who may be competent but nonrepresentative" (Chesney, 1978). This imperfect mobilization of participation presents HSAs, and our public institutions in general, with a representational dilemma—should they continue to rely upon "substantive representational" models, or is it important to restructure the processes of HSAs to provide a "demographically representative" body? Although it is impossible to evaluate the social benefits of this question completely without knowing the costs and consequences of structural change, an indication of the trade-offs and relative benefits between these methods of representation will be provided by looking at their contributions, within the context of HSAs, to the related issues of competence, commitment, and responsiveness.

Most consumer members of the NY–Penn HSA can be categorized as professional consumers. Despite their demographic bias, we have seen that these individuals as a group tend to articulate the general sentiments of the population but at the expense of the specific policy emphases of the most disadvantaged segments of the population. The question becomes whether this bias warrants the restructuring of the governing board, or does the membership of a substantive representational body promote other important planning values such as competency and commitment, which offsets this lack of total responsiveness to the community? A comparison of attendance and knowledge indicators for all SES groups and the observations of NY–Penn planners and staff who must work with these individuals will be utilized to provide some insights into any important differences between these groups which could affect the integrity of health planning.

NY–Penn planners and staff do express the belief that, in general, lower SES groups are not as well prepared for the rigors of health planning. They are, it is believed, less informed about the complexities of health problems, have more trouble understanding planning terminology and methodology, attend meetings with less frequency, and serve shorter lengths of stay on the planning board—contributing to high turnover and lack of continuity among their members.

According to the data, although 45 percent of all low-income participants report difficulties in comprehending technical and planning information, this percentage is no greater than that of any other consumer group. In fact, no income group has less than 40 percent of its membership expressing some difficulty. Low SES groups' knowledge of general health care issues, while not quite as good as other consumer members, is not dramatically inferior either (see Table 7.7). Thirty-six percent of the lowest income groups have at least a moderate understanding of health care issues in comparison to 43 percent and 50 percent for the two highest. (Interestingly, the $10,000 to $14,999 income group demonstrates the highest level of understanding—80 percent.) Based upon these sources, it is difficult to discern a significant pattern of planning incompetencies which can be solely attributed to low economic groups.

Attendance figures are also devoid of any systematic pattern relating to SES. This information, compiled by the NY–Penn HSA, demonstrates that low-income groups attend planning board meetings with just as much frequency—and in most cases more regularity—than consumer members of all others income categories. Furthermore, analyses of attendance which control for the effects of health care knowledge and level of understanding of technical planning information illustrate that a respondent's level of knowledge and/or understanding does not lead to any variation in one's planning commitment for any SES group. Groups possessing low levels of information and understanding are equally as active as better-informed groups. These findings suggest that some general sense of "civic responsibility" may account for the fact that planning commitments transcend knowledge and income levels. Since higher SES levels have generally been found to be associated with one's

Table 7.7
Knowledge Index for Consumers by Income Categories

Knowledge Index	Income			
	Under $10,000	$10,000- $14,999	$15,000- $24,999	$25,000 and over
None	18%	20%	27%	-
Little	45%	-	31%	50%
Moderate	18%	60%	35%	33%
Substantial	18%	20%	8%	17%
	N= 11	N= 5	N= 26	N= 13

Source: Information for this table was derived from the administration of questionnaires to consumer members on the governing board.
Note: This index is based upon the level of understanding of consumers for several health care problems. Dash represents 0% in this table and in Table 7.6.

civil orientation, this would explain both the concentration of consumer members within high SES groups and the uniform level of commitment among all groups.

In summary, representatives of the lower SES groups do not seem to exhibit any significant differences in planning competency or commitment. These findings do not suggest, however, that mandatory extension of the planning process to facilitate the notion of "descriptive representation" will automatically produce citizens who are equally as committed, knowledgeable, competent, and self-motivated. The success of this effort will rely to a great extent upon the method of selection that is required to achieve demographic goals. If self-selection mechanisms can be enhanced and perpetrated to satisfy these needs, then it is likely that self-motivated and interested individuals will be attracted. If these goals require the active solicitation of underrepresented groups, it is probable that the high levels of civil commitment which presently exist may decrease. Therefore, planning agencies would have to engage more actively in educational and motivational activities in order to maintain an equilibrium between the activities and competencies of various consumer members. Without prior knowledge of the consequences of expanding participation within the planning process, it is difficult to make any final determination in regard to the relative benefits of "demographic representation."

The fact that high SES groups do dominate the consumer contingent of health planning takes on renewed importance for planning in light of the findings of this study that not only are public activists drawn from different backgrounds but they do indeed articulate and emphasize values which differ from those of the general public. This strongly suggests that not only does the "simple extension of the opportunity to participate" fail to produce equal participation rates (Fagence, 1977:204), but in many cases it fails to promote popular equality. Public participation determines not only which groups are represented but, more importantly, what values will be articulated and counted.

Government officials have extended great amounts of time, money, and efforts to encourage a meaningful and substantive role for citizens in planning and administration. These programs, though far from perfect, have expanded the representativeness and perspectives traditionally encountered by planning structures.

REFERENCES

Alford, Robert 1975
>   *Health Care Politics: Ideological and Interest Group Barriers to Reform.* (Chicago: University of Chicago Press).

Bachrach, Peter, and Morton Baratz 1962
>   "Two Faces of Power," *American Political Science Review* 56:947–52.

—— 1963
"Decisions and Nondecisions: An Analytical Framework,"
American Political Science Review 57:632–42.

Bireland, Donald 1971
"Community Action Boards and Maximum Feasible Participation," *American Journal of Public Health* 61:293.

Chesney, James 1978
"Health Systems Agencies: Representation and Accountability."
Paper delivered at the Annual Meeting of the American Political
Science Association, New York, September.

Cupps, D. Stephen 1977
"Emerging Problems of Citizen Participation," *Public Administration Review* 37:478–87.

Eulau, Heinz, and Kenneth Prewitt 1973
*Labyrinths of Democracy: Adaptations, Linkages, Representation, and
Policies in Urban Politics.* (Indianapolis, Ind.: Bobbs-Merrill).

Fagence, Michael 1977
Citizen Participation in Planning. (New York: Pergamon Press).

Griffiths, A. P. 1960
"How Can One Person Represent Another?" *Aristotelian Society*
supp. vol. X:187–208.

Pennock, James Roland 1968
"Political Representation: An Overview," in James Roland Pennock and J. W. Chapman, eds., *Representation.* (New York: Atherton Press).

Pitkin, Hanna 1967
The Concept of Representation. (Berkeley: University of California
Press).

Riska, Elaine, and James Taylor 1978
"Consumer Attitudes Toward Health Policy and Knowledge
About Health Legislation," *Journal of Health, Politics, Policy, and
Law* 3:112–23.

U.S. Congress 1975
National Health Planning and Resources Development Act of 1974.
Pub. L. 93–641. 93rd Congress, Section 1512 c 1. (Washington,
D.C.: Government Printing Office).

Verba, Sidney, and Norman H. Nie 1972
Participation in America: Political Democracy and Social Equality. (New
York: Harper and Row).

8

The Role of Citizen-Initiated Programs in the Formulation of National Housing Policies

RACHEL G. BRATT

Over the past decade, the notion that local citizens have a better chance than the federal government of solving their own housing and community development problems has had a bipartisan appeal. A key principle of President Jimmy Carter's National Urban Policy was that "the potentially significant role of the neighborhood in city building and rebuilding efforts" must be recognized. The rationale for this was as follows:

Many neighborhood groups around the country have begun successful, innovative community planning and neighborhood revitalization activities. This trend should be encouraged by the Federal government. Neighborhood residents and groups are the ones affected most directly by revitalization efforts. They are the closest to some of the problems and often best able to judge what solutions will be most effective. No urban policy can succeed if it ignores the views of neighborhood people and groups and if it does not secure their continuous involvement in varied neighborhood improvement efforts. (HUD, 1978:121)

President Ronald Reagan's campaign rhetoric echoed some of his competitor's logic. In a speech before the National Urban League he pointed out that neighborhood-based revitalization efforts such as the Neighborhood Housing Services (NHS) program "are in the best American tradition" and that he would act aggressively to strengthen such initiatives (Neighborhood Reinvestment Corporation [NRC], 1981:3). Although President Reagan's Commission on Housing did not articulate a central position for neighborhood people, its report pointed out that many of the most innovative ideas in housing have been devised and implemented at the state and local level" (NRC, 1982:27).

While Reagan has fulfilled his campaign pledge to support the NHS program, his administration has virtually dismantled the burgeoning support for other types of neighborhood-based efforts. One of his first actions as president was to terminate the Neighborhood Self-Help Development program, enacted in 1978, which provided direct federal funding for citizen-initiated projects. To fill this void, the president has called for more voluntary participation and support from private corporations and local citizens.

During this period of low or no federal funding, we are in a good position (albeit a sad one) to assess the role that citizens have placed in initiating housing programs and to question whether these efforts can serve as models for additional programs replicated through a national agency—either federal or private. If a program is successful in one locale, is it possible to create similar programs in other parts of the country?

Viewed from a theoretical perspective, this paper examines prototype programs that involve "bottom-up" citizen participation—citizens, rather than government, must be the prime actor. Stuart Langton has made the distinction between this and "top-down" participation:

[C]itizen participation activities are initiated and controlled by two sources, citizens and government. Therefore, we can distinguish between two general types of citizen participation: citizen-initiated and government-initiated. This distinction is frequently made when people employ the euphemisms "bottom-up" and "top-down" to describe activities. (1978:21)

Although Langton views both as legitimate forms of participation, other analysts, such as Arnstein (1969), Pearlman (1978), and Gittell (1980) see top-down approaches as neither yielding true benefits to citizens nor redistributing resources or power. For example, according to Pearlman, "[I]t is only an active, well organized group with its own positive agenda and the ability to mobilize people and resources independently [that] can successfully change the way decisions are made or benefits are allocated in our society" (1978:66). This statement underscores the potential of bottom-up citizen participation. It suggests that public policies that encourage this type of participation would have a greater likelihood of benefiting individuals than policies not so designed. This chapter looks at several examples of how national programs have been modeled after local initiatives with a view toward better understanding how public policy could incorporate the elements of bottom-up programs. In order to appreciate the traditional way that the federal government has treated citizen involvement in its housing programs, a brief overview of past initiatives will be presented. Examples will be provided of how several bottom-up housing programs have served as models for significant national programs. The final section of the chapter offers some suggestions for how bottom-up efforts could be supported by the federal government and for how new locally based programs could be nurtured through top-down initiatives.

CITIZENS AND FEDERAL HOUSING PROGRAMS: A HISTORICAL OVERVIEW

Most of the U.S. government's housing programs stipulated little or no role for citizens other than as recipients, or users. From the 1930s to the late 1950s, the federal government pursued two main housing strategies. First, it stimulated the construction and rehabilitation of housing through direct loans (Farmers Home Administration) and through modernization and mortgage loan insurance programs (Federal Housing Administration (FHA) and Veterans' Administration). The second major federal approach to housing, the public housing program, involved the direct construction and management of multifamily developments through local housing authorities. At the heart of all these initiatives was the federal government's desire to stimulate the depression-era economy and provide employment opportunities. Housing, while a goal of the various pieces of legislation, was not the primary objective.[1] Despite this non-consumer orientation, the federal housing programs have still managed, overall, to provide some new opportunities and a decent quality of housing services to households with few or no options on the private market.[2]

During the late 1960s federal housing policy came under new pressures. Faced with racial unrest in scores of American cities, Congress enacted a series of new subsidy programs aimed at providing increased housing opportunities to low- and moderate-income people by encouraging greater private sector participation. Part of this strategy involved an explicit emphasis on extending federal housing assistance to deteriorated urban areas. But while citizen needs may have more squarely motivated this second generation of federal housing programs, citizen participation in those efforts was still neither expected nor required.

Despite the high hopes that surrounded the new programs, within a few years several had become the target of serious criticism. In January 1973, President Richard Nixon took a decisive step by declaring a housing moratorium and suspending virtually all the existing subsidy programs. What went wrong was the subject of numerous studies and investigations.[3]

Burned by an emphasis on new housing construction, it is not surprising that federal thinking began to shift to programs that depended on direct subsidies to households to lower rentals in the private housing market. The Section 8 existing housing program has, since its enactment in 1974, been the cornerstone of federal housing policy. To the extent that the current administration favors any subsidy approach, the direct cash voucher, modeled after Section 8, is clearly the favored strategy (Report of the President's Commission on Housing, 1982).

While residents have not had a mandated role in federal housing programs they, nevertheless, have not been passive bystanders. Faced with serious problems with their housing, many groups have organized to try to improve their living conditions. Some of the problems that stimulated resident activism actually grew out of dissatisfaction with the federal housing programs. Other problems that motivated citizens related to poor conditions in the low-cost private housing market—inadequate supply, abandonment of rental property, high costs, and low vacancy rates. But what we have today is a rich assortment of citizen-initiated programs that present important alternatives to the existing public and private ways of providing housing.

CITIZEN-INITIATED HOUSING PROGRAMS

Four types of citizen-initiated housing programs that have been or are being used as models for federal or other nationally oriented programs will be discussed below.[4] These are:

The Neighborhood Housing Services Program

Small-scale homeownership programs

Tenant management of public housing

Alternative management/ownership of private rental housing.

In each, there has been a similar progression from problem definition to program development and operation. A "model"—perhaps more idealized in some respects than the examples to be discussed below—of how citizen-initiated housing programs are created and operate incorporate the following steps.

- Serious housing need or problem is felt.
- Community or tenant group coalesces around the specific issue and puts together an action agenda.
- Group solicits and receives financial and technical supports from governmental bodies as well as from the private sector (banks, foundations, and businesses).
- Funding and other external supports are maintained or even increased after the program is launched.
- Resident control and participation are maintained throughout the life of the program.
- Significant consumer supports and safeguards are incorporated into the program.

If these steps are important for a successful bottom-up housing effort, how could they be built into or adapted to a national program? Although complete information about the original bottom-up programs and the replicated programs is not available, it is useful to question the extent to which the national programs appear to have been able to incorporate these components.[5]

Neighborhood Housing Services

Redlining, or the unwillingness of banks to lend in certain areas of the city, stimulated the most widely publicized citizen-initiated housing program. Neighborhood Housing Services (NHS), which started in a deteriorated, redlined section of Pittsburgh in 1968, was a resident-sponsored reinvestment program. Through the neighborhood's own assessment of its problems, a four-way partnership was forged between the residents; mortgage lenders; the city, which committed to undertake a code-enforcement program and promised much-needed public services; and a foundation which provided a high-risk pool of money for potential borrowers who were considered ineligible by the banks.

By most accounts, NHS has enjoyed considerable success.[6] Not only has it been credited with stabilizing the original Pittsburgh NHS Neighborhood (Ahlbrandt and Brophy, 1975), but it also has served as a model for scores of additional NHS programs. As federal officials became aware of the success of Pittsburgh's NHS, the Federal Home Loan Bank Board and HUD joined together to form the Urban Reinvestment Task Force, with the purpose of assisting other locales to develop their own NHS programs. This effort received full congressional support in 1978 with the enactment of the Neighborhood Reinvestment Corporation Act. By 1983 there were NHS organizations operating in 182 neighborhoods in 132 cities (Whiteside, 1983).

While all evaluations of the national NHS programs are now several years old, the early results have been encouraging. More than any other local program, Pittsburgh's NHS is responsible for the notion that local successes can translate into national programs. To the extent that the Neighborhood Reinvestment Corporation (NRC) appears to be duplicating these achievements, it seems clear that much of the reason lies in the ability of the national agency to repeat each of the key ingredients of the original Pittsburgh program. The roles of citizens, private lenders, and local governments are clearly described by NRC's guidelines (HUD, 1980). In addition, types of neighborhoods and housing stocks that are thought to be suitable for an NHS program are all carefully delineated. While this specificity may serve to exclude more neighborhoods that could benefit from the program, it also provides sufficiently detailed information for the community to launch a program. Overall, NRC has demonstrated that a local program can be replicated at the national level. It provides an important example of the viability of the approach and will be discussed further in the last section of the paper.

Small-Scale Homeownership Programs

The second group of citizen-initiated programs that prompted a national response were the small-scale homeownership programs. Faced with no homeownership opportunities for lower-income families coming through federal channels until the late 1960s, many community groups organized their own home-ownership programs. The sweat equity approach, which enables people to substitute their own labor for some or all of the downpayment on a home, has been a particularly important component of citizen-initiated homeownership programs.

Sweat equity programs have been in existence for over forty years. In 1945, an Indianapolis settlement house initiated a housing construction program known as Flanner House Homes, Inc. Between 1950 and 1965, 366 families were able to participate in the construction of their homes, with each family's work assessed at between 25 and 30 percent of the total value of the house. Similarly, in 1964, Better Rochester Living, Inc., offered homeownership opportunities to lower-income families, with rehabilitation work performed by the prospective owners in exchange for their down payment.

Yet, an evaluation of these programs pointed out that it takes a huge amount of administrative and other support services to make these efforts work. The four programs that were studied, including Flanner House Homes and Better Rochester Living "helped a combined total of about 500 poor families to buy homes, at a cost of thousands of devoted manhours of work, many of them unpaid" (Frieden and Newman, 1970). Similarly, HUD Secretary Robert Weaver noted that each homeownership program "requires a tremendous amount of assistance and aid by a nonprofit corporation. These are not volume programs. These are custom programs" (U.S. Subcommittee on Housing, 1968:126).

Fueled by the enthusiasm generated by these programs,[7] as well as a desire to find ways to quiet the urban unrest of the late 1960s, Congress, in 1968, enacted the first homeownership subsidy program. But while the federal government went so far as to borrow the "homeownership for the poor" idea from local communities, it did not follow some of the key aspects of the earlier programs. The Section 235 program was neither intended to be community-based nor did it include a specific role for prospective homeowners. The program was operated out of the HUD area office and local builders and developers were the key actors in its implementation. Even worse, the provision of counseling and other support services, which were so crucial to the success of the four innovative homeownership programs, was left up to voluntary agencies. Federally funded counseling services were not part of the Section 235 homeownership program (Bratt, 1976; U.S. Committee on Government Operations, 1976).

The final blow to the Section 235 program came when it was learned that many FHA officials had completely abandoned traditional underwriting practices, thereby allowing many blatantly ineligible households and many severely deficient homes to be approved for the program. In short, the 235 program was severely criticized for totally ignoring consumer needs and safeguards (U.S. Committee on Government Operations, 1976; HUD, 1973a).

As a result of these and many other defects, Section 235 eventually fell victim to the Nixon housing moratorium. While it managed to limp back onto the federal agenda after several years, it did so on a much reduced scale.[8] Thus, while the small-scale homeownership programs served as a partial stimulus for the federal effort, the government's failure to incorporate more closely the consumer protections and supportive structures of the local programs contributed to homeownership for low-income people falling into disfavor and being cheated of a fair test.

Tenant Management of Public Housing

Efforts by tenants to manage their own public housing developments have stimulated the third major citizen-initiated national housing program. Similar to the NHS experience, the original tenant-management model has resulted in several successfully replicated programs. Frustrated with poor conditions in some large public housing projects, tenants in several cities have organized tenant-management corporations. The best-known example of tenant-managed public housing developments is in St. Louis, Missouri. In that city, Tenant Management Corporations (TMCs) oversee the operation of more than 3,000 apartments in five family developments. Robert Kolodny has written:

An independent evaluation of the mature program has not been made, but there seems little question that the TMCs have mastered traditional real estate management. . . . They [the TMCs] have overseen substantial upgrading of the projects, which they inherited in an advanced state of under-occupancy and physical deterioration (1981a:137).

Another example of the takeover of management functions in a public housing development occurred in Newark, New Jersey. There, tenants launched a rent strike in a 1,200-unit development which resulted in a court-supervised agreement between tenants and the Newark Housing Authority which directed the latter to explore the possibility of a tenant management program (Diaz, 1979).[9]

Based on the experiences in St. Louis, as well as TMC programs in several other cities,[10] HUD, with the assistance of the Ford Foundation, launched a three-year demonstration of tenant management in 1976. The results of the national program appear to parallel those reported in St. Louis:

The National Tenant Management Demonstration has shown that management by tenants is a feasible alternative to conventional public housing management under certain conditions. In the majority of the demonstration sites, the tenant participants—all long-time residents of low-income public housing, most unemployed, and the majority black female family heads—mastered in three years the skills necessary to assume management responsibility for the housing developments in which they lived. . . .

The evaluation of tenant management on a series of measured standard performance indicators such as rent collection and the quality and timeliness of maintenance, shows that the residents were able to manage their developments as well as prior management had and, in so doing, to provide employment for some tenants and increase the overall satisfaction of the general resident population. (Manpower Demonstration Research Corporation, 1981:239)

An important characteristic of the demonstration was that it provided specific guidelines for the sites to follow. While some variation occurred, the basic model "closely paralleled the St. Louis effort. . . . [It] defined the nature of the TMC, the respective responsibilities of each partner, and the key events in which the TMC assumed operating responsibility" (Manpower Demonstration Research Corporation, 1981:21).

In assessing the experiences of the seven demonstration sites, the evaluators pointed out that three elements "work together to create the optimal conditions under which tenant management can flourish"—housing authority cooperation, strong tenant leadership, and carefully administered technical assistance and training (Manpower Demonstration Research Corporation, 1981:242). Yet, they also cautioned that the experience at one of the unsuccessful sites indicated that these elements are necessary but not always sufficient to ensure positive outcomes. And, finally, while the TMC demonstration was successful it was also very costly, but in terms of financial expenditures and individual time commitments from housing authority staff and the involved tenants. Thus, while it is clear that replication of the St. Louis TMC model was possible, it is also apparent that a simple formula that guarantees success is not yet (nor may it ever be) available.

Alternative Management/Ownership of Private Rental Housing

Increasingly, housing analysts from all political perspectives have begun to acknowledge that the private sector is ill-equipped to provide decent, low-cost housing. Even the President's Commission on Housing admitted that "the private market has been unwilling or unable to house many [low-income, single-parent, minority and large] families" (1982:31).

One of the ways in which the private sector is particularly vulnerable is to criticism in its inability or lack of desire to maintain vast quantities of older rental properties. Faced with dilapidated or abandoned buildings, residents and community people in several cities have implemented programs to salvage viable structures and return them to the housing stock under alternative management/ownership arrangements. Two such programs have stimulated national demonstrations: New York City's alternative management programs and Washington's Jubilee Housing.

New York City and the "510" Demonstration. It is not surprising that New York City, with the most abandoned buildings in the country, is the site of the most varied and comprehensive approaches for dealing with end-stage problems in the private housing stock. While some of New York's programs are administered through the city, much of the impetus for their creation came from tenant activities and neighborhood organization (Hartman et al., 1982).

Kolodny (1981a) has detailed seven programs that are known as the "alternative management programs." One of the most innovative, the Tenant Interim Lease Program, involves direct management by tenants of city-owned buildings (formerly privately owned and taken by the city because of unpaid taxes or other serious violations) if three-fifths of the residents sign a petition requesting it. After an eleven-month trial period, tenants are then offered the building as a tenant cooperative. The results have been encouraging: rent collections have averaged

90 percent compared to 63 percent for other city-managed properties, and tenant satisfaction has increased. Further, buildings in this program require a lower expenditure by the city than those managed centrally by city staff (Hurwitz, 1982). As of January 1, 1985, 130 buildings with 3,470 units had been sold to tenant cooperatives. An additional 293 buildings were being managed by residents with the hope that they would be converted to cooperatives (Kolodny, 1986).

New York City also has had considerable experience with two older, yet similar, programs: cooperative conversions and sweat equity rehabilitation. Both emerged as a result of severe tenant frustration with buildings that had been abandoned by the private sector, and both developed after tenants had initiated efforts to salvage their homes.

The cooperative conversion program, sanctioned and supported by the city, emerged "primarily in response to the demands of tenants who had sustained their buildings for a period themselves but who needed the financing to upgrade the buildings and the leverage to gain permanent control of them at nominal cost" (Kolodny, 1981a:56). Since no formal evaluation of the program has been done, it is unknown exactly how many buildings have been converted and how successful they have been. One estimate is that there have been fewer than fifty such conversions (Sumka and Blackburn, 1982). Yet, Kolodny has offered the following summation:

Although many projects apparently failed, others prospered in very unlikely circumstances. [In the coops that are doing well] all the basic indicators of effective management are there: low vacancy rates, limited turnover, long waiting lists, good building maintenance, and general resident satisfaction. (1981a:57–58)

The successes of many of these initiatives are particularly noteworthy in view of the lack of any organized system of support for tenants. While "it was not surprising that many could not hold on and sustain what they had started [,] . . . the potential for a large-scale mutual aid strategy represented by these efforts was impressive" (Kolodny, 1986).

A nonprofit agency, the Urban Homesteading Assistance Board (UHAB), has been pivotal in sustaining and encouraging both sweat equity and conversion programs in New York. Established in 1974, UHAB provides tenant and community groups with technical assistance and support, in addition to acting as an intermediary between the city and the citizen-initiated project.

Despite the overall optimism, problems do exist. Building tenant and community management capacity is often a slow, difficult process and it is not yet known whether long-term tenant or community ownership will be achieved. At the very least, however, these programs have made three important contributions: they have provided options for low-income people who are desperate for decent housing, they have enabled community residents and tenants to gain valuable experience in housing management, and they were a major stimulus for a federal response.

The "510 demo," which derived its legal authority from the 1978 amendments to the 1970 Housing Act, authorized HUD to determine the feasibility of expanding homeownership opportunities in urban areas, giving special attention to the use of multifamily housing. Seven cities were chosen to carry out multifamily rehabilitation projects. Under the direct control of the city, private developers and community groups jointly rehabilitated buildings which were then transferred to cooperative or condominium ownership. Unlike the original model pioneered in New York, this demonstration did not include sweat equity. Instead, it depended on Section 8 or other subsidies to lower the ultimate costs to the occupants. In addition, the 510 demonstration defined a complex relationship for the developer and the community group and provided the former with some financially lucrative incentives to gain their involvement.

A recent evaluation of the 510 demo concluded that none of the demonstration projects was an unqualified success. Even in the most successful project, low-income cooperative ownership could only be achieved with subsidies for nearly two-thirds of the development costs and long-term Section 8 subsidies for a majority of tenants (Sumka, 1984). Yet, on balance, the report concluded:

[T]he 510 demonstrations showed that a developer-community group partnership could be made to work. . . . It also showed that low-income cooperatives can be created to the benefit of the residents of inner-city neighborhoods . . . but that such projects will not bear fruit without the considerable effort and dedication of the program staff. (Sumka, 1984)

One of the reasons for the mixed outcome may also be because the 510 demo was not as careful in promulgating detailed guidelines as were some of the other national programs discussed earlier. With a change from the Carter to the Reagan administration just as the demonstration was getting underway, there was significant pressure to get the program out of HUD as quickly as possible.

In a second HUD demonstration, also partially based on the New York experience, six cities were selected to undertake sweat equity rehabilitation programs. Sumka and Blackburn (1982) found that the results of the demonstration were mixed with only two cities establishing ongoing multifamily homesteading programs.

Thus, while it is significant that HUD attempted to replicate locally initiated ideas, it is possible that the multifamily sweat equity and cooperative conversion programs may not be as easy to adapt and replicate as the Neighborhood Housing Services program, which applies to single family homes. Or, it also may be that an adequate test of the concept has not yet been launched. Sumka and Blackburn have proposed several requirements which seem to be essential components of cooperative conversion programs.

Self-help labor and the elimination of profit and overhead can only go so far. Acquisition costs, material purchases, property taxes, interest on debt, maintenance, and utilities will continue to contribute to carrying costs. Without additional subsidies, these may be beyond the financial capacity of homesteaders. Besides financial support, there is also a continuing need for technical assistance. Most community groups and tenant organizations enter the homesteading process without the essential legal, architectural, financial or managerial skills. Training and technical assistance are necessary to assure their success.

With proper attention to these details, multifamily homesteading holds out the possibility of being an important mechanism for bringing a substantial number of decaying dwelling units back into useful service. For many of these properties in older declining neighborhoods, this may be the only feasible approach, given their unprofitability for private investors. (1982:107)

Whether multifamily housing is inherently more difficult to work with than single family homes, or whether the true potential for alternative management/ownership strategies for buildings that were formerly privately owned has not yet been realized, early results of the national demonstrations suggest that replication of the original efforts is far from straightforward.

Jubilee Housing. The second citizen-initiated program that is aimed at upgrading and maintaining older private rental units for use by low-income tenants and that has been the model for a national program is Washington's Jubilee Housing. Unlike all of the other national demonstrations that have been described, marketing of the "Jubilee model" has no federal involvement. In this case, a private foundation was specifically set up to help stimulate the creation of Jubilee-type programs in cities across the country.

Starting in the early 1970s, several groups, or missions, of Washington's Church of the Saviour began addressing the needs of the poor in the church's neighborhood, the Adams-Morgan section. Housing was one issue that surfaced as being particularly problematic. Church members articulated a goal to provide decent, safe, affordable, permanent housing for very low income people.

In 1973 Jubilee Housing was incorporated as a nonprofit group. After leasing its first two buildings, it began a massive rehabilitation program. By 1979, Jubilee had acquired six buildings with a total of 213 units. The only federal money that Jubilee received was a $1.8 million HUD innovative grant which, along with private donations, supported much of the rehabilitation costs. Tenants are involved in the management of the buildings, which rent at substantially below market prices and plans have begun to transfer some of the buildings to cooperative ownership. By providing health, employment, and educational programs, the Jubilee approach is aimed at dealing with a host of needs and problems facing lower-income people.

Jubilee involves a complex set of relationships with the private sector including loans, grants, and donations of manpower. Its most significant private support comes from James Rouse, a well-known developer and entrepreneur. In 1978 Rouse organized a group of private business people and professionals to provide technical assistance and advice to Jubilee whenever necessary. As more and more people became aware of Jubilee and Rouse's commitment to private/neighborhood-based revitalization, Rouse decided to spend his "retirement years" devoted to implementing this process elsewhere. In 1980 Rouse created two new entities, the Enterprise Development Corporation (EDC) and the Enterprise Foundation. EDC is a wholly owned for-profit subsidiary of the foundation. In addition to capital generated by EDC, Rouse has managed to raise more than $15 million from private corporations and foundations.

The Enterprise Foundation is currently supporting housing groups and helping to establish local private sector support groups in a number of cities across the country. A small staff of foundation field workers are responsible for providing on-site technical assistance to local groups and advising them about how to enlist the support of the local business community and how to adapt the Jubilee model to the needs of their own neighborhood.

Whether or not Washington's Jubilee will manage to achieve its lofty goals and whether or not the Jubilee model will be reproducible in other cities remains to be seen. However, for the present, it is sufficient to note that Jubilee represents another example of a citizen-initiated housing program that is in the process of being replicated at the national level.

CONCLUSIONS AND POLICY IMPLICATIONS

Two broad conclusions are possible from this study. First, citizen-initiated housing programs have provided some clear benefits to people suffering with various housing problems. Second, national programs have borrowed these ideas with varying degrees of success. The preceding analysis suggests that there are five critical, although not necessarily sufficient, ingredients for the successful replication of a citizen-initiated activity.

1. *Role of Community*

It is essential that any top-down effort be sensitive to the fact that the program's roots and initial success were in a bottom-up process. Therefore, in replicating a program it is critical for the national agency to locate a competent and committed group of citizens with which to work. The community or tenant group must be assured of considerable autonomy and control of the program. Extreme care must be taken by the national agency to insure that the replicated program is viewed as being part of the community, as well as for the community.

2. *Guidelines*

The national agency must provide specific guidelines and on-site technical assistance and support. It must evaluate why the original program worked and what the key components are and clearly devise an implementation plan. It must then be prepared to "beat the bushes" for suitable sites and painstakingly support local efforts to grapple with the model and apply it to the locales' own situations.

3. *Public and Private Cooperation*

The national guidelines must also carefully spell out a role for public and private actors in the community. Cooperation among local agencies and individuals is a key characteristic of successful citizen-initiated housing programs. In addition, the availability of technical assistance from the local community is a critical resource to housing groups.

4. *Funding and Technical Assistance*

Adequate financial resources and technical assistance must be made available to the community group to plan, implement, and maintain the program. Insufficient funding or assistance in any of these phases may severely hamper the program's viability.

5. *Consumer Safeguards*

All the citizen-initiated programs studied share a common thread: they all have, as their primary concern and responsibility, shelter and neighborhood improvement. Unlike most federal programs that are laden with multiple goals, citizen-initiated housing programs directly address consumer needs. The agency responsible for replicating a local program must make sure that needed safeguards and consumer assistance are provided.

While the above are suggested as important components of a successful replication process, there is still much that is not fully understood. The ability to replicate citizen-initiated programs would be improved if we had answers to the following.

1. What type of local housing programs can be replicated?

2. Under what circumstances does the most effective replication take place? To what extent does the national program have to follow the guidelines of the local program? To what extent should local circumstances allow the model to be altered, rather than abandoning it altogether?

3. How can the top-down function of government (or some other body) to replicate the program be balanced by the need for citizens to be involved as a bottom-up-type activity?

Even without answers to these questions, two policy recommendations emerge from this analysis. Since we know that good national programs can evolve from local initiatives, public policy should be geared toward facilitating this process.

(1)*Federal funding is needed to encourage local initiatives and experimentation*. The best model for such a policy is the Neighborhood Self-Help Development Act. Enacted in 1978, this legislation, in the pre-Reagan years, provided funding directly to 124 community groups engaged in a wide array of neighborhood development activities. Funding for this program should be reinstated. But in order for this policy to have maximum effectiveness, a companion public policy is needed.

(2)*The federal government should aggressively seek those successful local policies that appear to be reproducible and then market them nationally*. New legislation for this activity also is not needed. The Neighborhood Reinvestment Corporation may be well suited for this function. Its legislative mandate calls for it to

[provide] grants and technical assistance to select neighborhood preservation projects which show promise as mechanisms for reversing neighborhood decline and improving the quality of neighborhood life. . . . The corporation shall experimentally replicate neighborhood preservation projects which have demonstrated success, and after creating reliable developmental processes, bring the new programs to neighborhoods throughout the United States.[11]

However, the NCR presently supports only activities that complement ongoing NHS programs. The current operation of its Neighborhood Preservation Program is neither involved with looking for innovative programs that are being carried out in non-NHS neighborhoods nor in replicating efforts that may be suitable for non-NHS neighborhoods.

The above proposal would enable the NRC and HUD to broaden their focus and to encourage locales to implement top-down housing programs that are based on the experiences of successful bottom-up programs. The effectiveness of this approach would signal a new meaning and an actual interdependence between the two types of citizen participation. Bottom-up citizen-initiated efforts could be used as the model and rationale for public bodies to replicate similar activities. This would then create a top-down citizen participation process that would be based explicitly on the actual needs and aspirations of the community and would be dependent on continued citizen involvement.

The theoretical possibility of such a program working, is, however, overshadowed by the unlikelihood of it being adopted. If Arnstein (1969:222) is correct that "since those who want power normally want to hang onto it, . . . it has . . . to be wrested by the powerless rather than proffered by the powerful," the chance of government creating a program to support bottom-up initiatives would appear to be minimal without a groundswell of citizen demands for such a program. This conclusion reinforces the view that government does not serve the interests of those who are most in need and does not enhance equal access to resources and opportunities. Instead, the government's reluctance to embrace wide-scale experimentation and support of bottom-up models provides further evidence that government serves other functions, such as those outlined by O'Connor (1973) and others: to legitimize itself and to enhance the private accumulation of capital.

NOTES

1. See, for example, Marcuse, 1978.
2. For a recent assessment of the federal public housing program see Bratt, 1986a.

3. See Downs, 1972; Report of the Task Force on Improving the Operation of Federally Insured or Financed Housing Programs, 1972; and HUD, 1973a.

4. Two local government-initiated, as opposed to citizen-initiated, programs which also prompted national demonstrations will not be discussed in this paper. The Apartment Improvement Program, which originated in Yonkers, New York, has become an important model for other such programs and is administered through the Neighborhood Reinvestment Corporation. The second program, modeled after urban homesteading programs in Wilmington, Delaware, and Baltimore, Maryland, prompted a major federal program that was legislated by Section 810 of the Housing and Community Development Act of 1974.

5. The descriptions of most of the following programs are revised from Bratt, 1986b. The material on Jubilee Housing was revised from a section of a report by Bratt, Byrd, and Hollister, 1983. Bratt 1986b also contains information on several community-based housing programs, not being discussed here because they did not serve as models for national programs.

6. While the NHS concept has wide appeal, it has also been the target of criticism. For example, critics have charged that some of the selected NHS neighborhoods had not been severely deteriorated and that, mot likely, they would have been rehabilitated without public assistance. Furthermore, opponents have pointed out that when a bank becomes involved with an NHS, it may feel justified in neglecting other inner city areas and that it has, essentially, "paid its dues" to the community.

7. In 1967, Senator Percy sponsored a bill that would have created a National Home Ownership Foundation. While the bill was eventually voted down, largely for political reasons (see Bratt, 1976), witnesses who were called to testify on the benefits of homeownership to lower-income people included several representatives of the demonstration programs (U.S. Congress, Senate, 1967).

8. In the aftermath of the Section 235 homeownership subsidy program, several community organizations again attempted to develop homeownership opportunities for lower-income residents. Homeowners Rehab, Inc., in Cambridge, Massachusetts, and the Worcester Cooperation Council's Home Improvement Program in Worcester, Massachusetts, initiated variations on the earlier sweat equity programs. Similar to their predecessors, these programs operate on extremely small scales: less than a dozen families per year are assisted through each agency (Siegenthaler, 1980).

9. Kolodny (1981a) points out that rent strikes were actually launched

in two public housing developments. However, tenants at one site refused to assume management responsibility.

10. For an overview of other early tenant management programs in public housing, see Diaz, 1979.

11. Neighborhood Reinvestment Corporation Act, Housing and Community Development Amendments of 1978, Public Law 95–557. 92 Stat. 2117. Sec. 606(a)(2) and (3).

REFERENCES

Ahlbrandt, Roger S., and Paul C. Brophy 1975
    Neighborhood Revitalization. (Lexington, Mass.: Lexington Books).
Arnstein, Sherry 1969
    "A Ladder of Citizen Participation," *American Institute of Planners Journal* 35:7:216–24.
Bratt, Rachel G. 1976
    "Federal Homeownership Policy and Home Finance: A Study of Program Operations and Impacts on the Consumer." Unpublished Ph.D. dissertation, MIT, Cambridge, Mass.
——— 1986a
    "Public Housing: The Controversy and Contribution," in Rachel Bratt, Chester Hartman, and Ann Meyerson, eds., *Critical Perspectives on Housing*. (Philadelphia: Temple University Press).
——— 1986b
    "Community-Based Housing Programs: Overview and Assessment," in Stuart Langton and James Peterson, eds., *Self-Help in America*. (Lexington, Mass.: Lexington Books).
Bratt, Rachel G., Janet M. Byrd, and Robert M. Hollister 1983
    "The Private Sector and Neighborhood Preservation." Prepared under contract to the Office of Policy Development and Research. U.S. Department of Housing and Urban Development, No. 7180–82, January.
Diaz, William, A. 1979
    "Tenant Management: An Historical and Analytical Overview." (New York: Manpower Demonstration Research Corporation).
Downs, Anthony 1972
    "Federal Housing Subsidies: Their Nature and Effectiveness and What We Should Do About Them." (Washington, D.C.: National Association of Home Builders and National Center for Housing Management, Inc.).
Frieden, Bernard J., and Jo-Ann Newman 1970
    "Home Ownership for the Poor?" *Trans-Action*, 8:47–53.

Gittell, Marilyn 1980
    The Limits of Citizen Participation. (Beverly Hills, Calif.: Sage
    Publications).
Hartman, Chester, Dennis Keating, and Richard LeGates 1982
    Displacement: How to Fight It. (Berkeley, Calif.: National Housing
    Law Project).
HUD. See U.S. Department of Housing and Urban Development.
Hurwitz, Ani 1982
    "New Alternatives for City-Owned Property," *City Limits*, 2:10–
    14.
Kolodny, Robert 1981a
    Multi-Family Housing: Treating the Existing Stock (Washington,
    D.C.: National Association of Housing and Redevelopment Of-
    ficials).
———— 1981b
    "Self-Help Can Be an Effective Tool in Housing the Urban Poor,"
    Journal of Housing, 6:135–42.
———— 1986
    "The Emergence of Self-Help as a Housing Strategy for the Ur-
    ban Poor," in Bratt, Hartman, and Meyerson, eds., *Critical Per-
    spectives on Housing.*(Philadelphia: Temple University Press).
Langton, Stuart 1978
    "What is Citizen Participation?" in Langton, ed., *Citizen Partic-
    ipation in America.* (Lexington, Mass.: Lexington Books).
Manpower Demonstration Research Corporation 1981
    *Tenant Management, Findings from a Three-Year Experiment in Pub-
    lic Housing.* (Cambridge, Mass.: Ballinger).
Marcuse, Peter 1978
    "Housing Policy and the Myth of the Benevolent State," *Social
    Policy*, 16:21–26.
Neighborhood Reinvestment Corporation 1981
    Program Report. "Partnerships for Vital Neighborhoods."
    (Washington, D.C.: Neighborhood Reinvestment Corp.).
O'Connor, James 1973
    The Fiscal Crisis of the State. (New York: St. Martin's Press).
Pearlman, Janice 1978
    "Grassroots Participation from Neighborhood to Nation," in
    Stuart Langton, ed., *Citizen Participation in America.* (Lexington,
    Mass.: Lexington Books).
Report of the President's Commission on Housing 1982
    Washington, D.C.

Report of the Task Force on Improving the Operation of Federally
    Insured or Financed Housing Programs 1972
    Vols. I, II & III. Under contract to HUD, No. H-2017R.
Siegenthaler, Mark 1980
    "Work Equity and Housing Assistance Projects." Unpublished
    M.A. thesis, Department of Urban and Environmental Policy,
    Tufts University, Medford, Mass.
Sumka, Howard, 1984
    "Factors Influencing the Success of Low-Income Cooperatives."
    Unpublished manuscript prepared for presentation at the An-
    nual Meeting of the Association of Collegiate Schools of Plan-
    ning, New York.
Sumka, Howard J., and Anthony J. Blackburn 1982
    "Multifamily Urban Homesteading: A Key Approach to Low-
    Income Housing," *Journal of Housing*, 39:104–7.
U.S. Congress. House. Committee on Government Operations 1972
    "Defaults on FHA-Insured Mortgages (Detroit)." Hearings Be-
    fore a Subcommittee. 92nd Congress, 1st sess.
———— House. Subcommittee on Housing of the Committee on Bank-
    ing and Currency 1968
    "Housing and Urban Development Legislation and Urban In-
    surance." Hearings. 90th Congress, 2d sess., part 1.
———— Senate. Subcommittee on Housing and Urban Affairs of the
    Committee on Banking and Currency 1967
    "Housing Legislation of 1967." Hearings. 90th Congress, 1st
    Sess., part 2.
U.S. Department of Housing and Urban Development 1973a
    "Housing in the Seventies."
———— 1973b
    "Report on Internal Audit of HUD Single Family Ap-
    praisal/Inspection Procedures and Mortgagees' Loan Processing
    Activities." Office of Inspector General, Office of Audit. No.
    05–2–4001–0000. (Washington, D.C.: Government Printing Of-
    fice).
———— 1978
    "The President's National Urban Policy Report." (Washington,
    D.C.: Government Printing Office).
———— 1980
    *Creating Local Partnerships: The Role of the Urban Reinvestment Task
    Force in Developing Neighborhood Housing Services Organizations.*
    Office of Policy Development and Research. Washington, D.C.

Whiteside, William A. 1983
    Statement submitted to the House Banking, Finance and Urban
    Affairs Subcommittee on Housing and Community Develop-
    ment. "Administration's Housing Authorization Proposals for
    Fiscal Year 1984."

9

Technocratic versus Democratic Options for Educational Policy

EDWARD P. MORGAN

Of the many areas of public policy, public education has probably the longest record of tension between technocratic and democratic values. Indeed, the history of public education is replete with tensions between two pairs of dichotomies: lay (or citizen) versus professional (or expert) control of educational decision making, and localism versus centralization in educational governance. While these are theoretically distinct dichotomies, they have been linked in most educational policy struggles. Citizen control and localism have most often reflected the democratic model of educational governance—in particular the value of accountability—while expert decision making and centralization have reflected the technocratic model and the value of efficiency.

From its origins in the mid-nineteenth century, public education has been steeped in democratic rhetoric. "Disinterested amateurs" and the local community played a critical role in shaping the common school. Gradually, with impetus from the Progressive movement and "scientific management," education became increasingly bureaucratized, centralized, and professionalized. Some argue convincingly that the history of education has, in fact, been one of gradual bureaucratic entrenchment (Katz, 1971) and centralization (Cronin, 1973).

Despite the apparent dominance of the technocratic model of educational decision making, tensions between the two models have persisted, in part because the values of democracy continue to be compelling. At two points in the past twenty years, the democratic model has provided a framework for major challenges to mainstream educational governance. In the late 1960s the community control movement attacked the city school bureaucracy for its unresponsiveness to the needs and demands of inner-city, minority populations; simultaneously, a more libertarian critique of "schooling" was launched, arguing that bureaucratic schools generally were stifling and antieducational.

The school bureaucracies responded to these critiques by adopting such policies as school decentralization, open classrooms, and magnet or alternative schools. Arguably, however, these policies represented a technocratic way of accommodating the democratic values of collective or individual accountability put forward by the community control movements and libertarian critiques.[1] For the most part, public education has continued to reflect the technocratic model and its correlates, centralization, bureaucracy, and standardization, through the continuing regionalization of rural schools, the closing of many city neighborhood schools, citywide and metropolitan desegregation, computerized learning, and competency testing.

Nonetheless, public satisfaction with schools has declined (Gallup, 1980), parental frustrations have led to an increase in private school attendance, and general dissatisfaction with the quality or cost of public services has been linked to a "taxpayers' revolt."[2] In addition, alarming rates of truancy, vandalism, and violence, particularly in urban schools, may be interpreted as evidence of widespread student alienation.

The principal heirs of the 1960s' critiques have been the citizen participation movement (and more radical, collectivist efforts) and the libertarian advocacy of policies like educational vouchers. The citizen participation movement is, in fact, an outgrowth of federal policies during the Johnson administration (broadened to include a vast array of public interest and environmental groups). In the area of education, citizen participation reflects the democratic objective of enhancing the input of lay participants (particularly largely excluded, low-income parents) in educational decision making. In effect, it views public dissatisfaction as evidence of the lack of accountability in educational policy making.

Most recently, the Reagan administration has tapped and given direction to public dissatisfaction through its "New Federalism" policies. By reducing federal funding for categorical grants, emphasizing state and local decision making through a block grant structure, and supporting private education through proposed tuition tax credits, the New Federalism stresses various ways of making public education more accountable to individual consumers and divergent localities. (Other aspects of Reagan's educational policies, such as deregulation, have been advocated in the name of efficiency. This claim will be discussed below.)

It would appear, then, that both the New Federalism and the citizen participation movement reflect democratic thrusts against the predominance of technocratic decision making in education and other policy fields. I will assess the degree to which these policy movements do, in fact, represent a democratic challenge to technocratic decision making, I will attempt to distinguish the principal differences between them, and I will evaluate the current and potential balance between technocratic and democratic models.

In order to assess both the New Federalism and the citizen participation movement, it will be helpful to clarify the theoretical or value underpinnings of each. To do this, it is necessary to consider two value dimensions: efficiency-accountability and equality-liberty. Most educational policy approaches have reflected various combinations of these values. While the citizen participation movement and the New Federalism appear to share roots in the democratic emphasis on accountability, they diverge clearly on the equality-liberty dimension. In effect, they represent two of four distinct educational policy approaches or ideologies.

TECHNOCRACY AND DEMOCRACY: THE EFFICIENCY-ACCOUNTABILITY DIMENSION

Technocratic and democratic models of educational governance reflect basic tensions within the family of liberal-democratic values—technocracy representing the liberal emphasis on universalism, democracy the more particularistic emphasis on participation. As applied to education, the technocratic model subscribes to an emphasis on bureaucratic organization as a means of maximizing efficiency, professional autonomy to enhance productivity through expertise, and rational decision making as a procedure for institutional effectiveness. The democratic model, on the other hand, has stressed the twin objectives of citizen or lay control and localism. We may briefly consider the normative foundation of both expert-citizen and centralization-localism dichotomies as applied to education.

Expert Versus Citizen

In emphasizing the role of the expert, the technocratic model rests on four assumptions about public education: (1) education is inherently rational and universal and thus can be standardized, (2) the most efficient mode of learning is through instruction by experts in a given subject matter (and presumably in effective pedagogical techniques), (3) learning proceeds in a building-block manner and thus can be ordered in progressive steps, and (4) educational institutions can evaluate learning outcomes by quantified, comparative measures.

The democratic side of the expert-citizen dichotomy counters these premises by asserting that (1) education is also subjective and particular and thus must reflect the interests, motivations, and needs of diverse individual learners; (2) while instruction, or external direction, is a necessary component of meaningful learning, an empathy for the internal world of the student is equally critical (more radical libertarians would, of course, argue that the internal world of the learner is all that is necessary for education to take place; the external world is a given, to be explored according to the needs and motivations of each learner); (3) although learning involves cumulative levels of sophistication, intellectual development cannot be packaged in a standardized manner for all learners; (4) while performance measurements are useful for institutional purposes, even if biased, they do not accurately reflect the range of valuable educational outcomes produced by learning experiences (these include some that are subjective and noncomparable).

As a result of its normative orientations, the democratic model asserts that lay citizens, including learners, have a quality of "expertise" that must play a significant role in shaping educational policies. In effect, the "citizen" side of the dichotomy views education as something that is inherently political since it must reflect the subjective world of learners and the values of parents. Much of the thrust of professionalization in education, on the other hand, has been linked to an effort to "take politics out of education."

Centralization Verus Localism

The other dichotomy found in the tension between technocratic and democratic models of education reflects the organizational implications of each side of the expert-citizen dichotomy. Centralization is a means of organizing the universal function as education in an efficient manner. Given the premise of standardized learning, and the goal of liberating young people from narrowing, subjective limitations, educational policy contains a built-in impetus toward increasing centralization (the ultimate is, of course, universal citizenship and a world curriculum).

On the other hand, an educational ideology which emphasizes the importance of diverse circumstances, needs, and interests places greater stress on ties between the school and the local community, whether those ties be racial, ethnic, or religious. Localism, in short, reflects the value of regional and cultural pluralism and a preference for smaller-scale institutions, face-to-face relations between parents and teachers, and a sense of community belongingness. Mirroring these values, education in the United States rests on constitutional origins that place the responsibility on states and localities rather than the federal government.

EQUALITY AND LIBERTY: THE EVOLUTION OF POLICY IDEOLOGIES

In theory, the movement toward centralization has largely been associated with the technocratic goal of efficiency, while the tradition of localism has been associated with the democratic goal of accountability. In actual fact, however, the tendency toward centralization may be more strongly associated with policies designed to enhance equal educational opportunity, while localism has long defended in the name of liberty—or "freedom from outside interference."

Public education plays a central role in a liberal democracy by contributing to equal life chances for all and by liberating the young from restrictive circumstances and empowering them to make the best of their abilities as adult citizens. With the implied emphasis on universalism and meritocracy, this educational function has gone hand-in-hand with such technocratic devices as standardized curricula and performance measures, professional impartiality, and integration. In order to attain these goals universally, educational policy making has shifted to higher levels of government and thus has become more centralized.

In effect, the emphasis on equality has become associated in practice with the technocratic model of educational governance, a combination that expresses the essence of liberal ideology in American politics. However, this is only one of two fundamental approaches to equality; the other is represented by the citizen participation movement (at least that aspect that concentrates on the empowerment of lower-income groups). Thus we may discern both a technocratic (liberal) and democratic (participatory or radical) version of educational equality.

Much of the centralization in educational policy making has come in the form of new interventions by government in educational operations. State requirements for standardized curricula, teacher certification, and mandated special programs for needy pupils have restricted the freedom of local school districts to operate as they please. Similarly, federal intervention in the form of school lunch programs, categorical aid for needy pupils, and court-ordered desegregation has imposed new requirements on both state and local policymakers.

As a consequence, the resistance to centralization, usually labeled conservative, has often had the effect of downplaying the emphasis on equality and elevating the value of liberty—of local or consumer freedom of choice. For the most part, this position has simply advocated less centralization and less of an emphasis on egalitarian policies, while remaining loyal to the technocratic stress on efficiency, professionalism, and bureaucratic organization. Such a policy approach might be called neo-conservative; moderate levels of compensatory education, for example, would be viewed as an acceptable approach toward enhancing educational equality without sacrificing either professional expertise or substantial local policy making.

However, with the advent of the Reagan administration (in particular, the emergence of the Libertarian party and the New Right) one can discern a fundamental disenchantment with technocratic offshoots like standardization and bureaucracy—in effect, a different brand of "romantic" conservatism. As the Reagan administration juggles conflicting constituencies, it is not surprising that the New Federalism places greater emphasis on liberty (a conservative de-emphasis on equality) while trying to balance the technocratic value of efficiency with the democratic value of accountability.

At the theoretical level, then, we may distinguish four models of ideologies of educational policy and governance, illustrated in Figure 9.1 Each combines two values from the efficiency-

Figure 9.1
Policy Ideologies

	Efficiency ("Technocratic")	Accountability ("Democratic")
Equality (More public intervention)	Liberal	Participatory
Liberty (Less public intervention)	Neo-Conservative	Romantic Conservative

accountability and equality-liberty dimensions. As such, the four ideologies provide a framework for evaluating various policy approaches. In considering the citizen participation movement and the New Federalism, however, it is readily apparent that actual policies embody the conflicting strains of more than one ideology.

THE CITIZEN PARTICIPATION CHALLENGE

With ideological roots in the political activism of the 1960s, citizen participation has taken many forms—from the short-lived community control movement to community organizing, the proliferation of public interest groups, court-mandated citizen advisory councils, and the like. While these forms of citizen participation vary widely in their functions, characteristics of their participants, and the degree of participant input policy decisions, they embrace the fundamental democratic values of accountability and equality. In order to evaluate the effectiveness of the citizen participation movement, it is necessary to examine both objectives.

First, citizen participation reflects the norm that policies, or more generally, government, should be responsive to the views of policy constituents or clients. At the same time, much of the impetus for citizen participation has come from an effort to redress inequalities in the policy process. Even the largely upper-middle-class public interest movement reflects a desire to counterbalance interests that are perceived as having an unfair edge in policy decisions (for example, "Big Business"). In its more radically democratic form, citizen participation is an effort to empower groups that have relatively little or no influence in formulating or implementing public policy—in short, to redistribute power.

While the two objectives, accountability and equality, tend to go hand-in-hand in actual practice, it is helpful to distinguish between them for analytical purposes. In short, we may distinguish between citizen-expert tensions inherent in the policy process, and broader concerns of political inequality. In both respects, the citizen participation movement has had at best limited success.

Citizen-Expert Tensions

An overview of citizen participation in education reveals that lay input into educational policy is sharply limited. In their study of a national sample of school districts, Tucker and Zeigler (1980) distinguished three types of democratic responsiveness: "preference responsiveness" (close parallels between the policy *preference* of the public and officials), "congruence responsiveness" (parallels between policy preferences of the public and policy *behavior* of officials) and "representational responsiveness" (correspondence between actual policy *demands* made by the public and the policy behavior of officials). In democratic terms citizen participation embraces all three types of responsiveness. Tucker and Zeigler, however, found ample evidence of only preference responsiveness in their sample of school districts, and their public opinion sample was skewed toward higher socio-economic groups. In general, there was little evidence of effective public input into educational policy decisions.[3]

To a considerable degree, this finding reflects the extent to which bureaucratization and the technocratic model discussed earlier prevail in education.[4] At the same time, however, it is important to recognize ways in which the citizen participation movement has made significant inroads into technocratic policy making.

There are many examples of citizen efforts that have enhanced lay input into educational policy making.[5] Two of the more common types of citizen participation are citizen advisory councils and advocacy groups; the former are often established at the school-district or school-site level by state and federal mandate, while the latter often reflect the spontaneous efforts of indigenous groups to protect the interests of identifiable groups of pupils, for example, minority or low-income children and those with handicaps.

Although it is fair to say that these citizen participation structures have generally failed to live up to their promise, studies of successful cases provide insights into effective participation (Davies et al., 1979; Clasby, 1979; Moore and Weitzman, 1981; Winecoff, 1982). As citizen participation takes on a group form—either through the organization of advocacy groups or formalized advisory councils—effectiveness depends on the quality of interaction between the group and school officials, within the group, and between the group and its constituencies. These, in turn, require (1) adequate resources (often a precondition for other requirements), (2) access to and the articulate presentation of accurate information about the school system, (3) responsive school officials, and (4) attention to organization building and close communication with constituencies.

Effective citizen participation has implications beyond mere policy input or the monitoring of policy implementation. In fact, evidence about "effective schools" seems to indicate that active involvement on the part of parents and students is an essential ingredient in enhancing learning as well as fostering a constructive school atmosphere.[6] Leadership by the school principal is one key factor, for he or she sets the tone and style for interaction among the many school participants. Opportunities for student participation and responsibility are also significant, as are staff expectations for pupil success.

Because effective participation requires responsiveness by school officials and staff, careful attention needs to be given to personnel recruitment and training, and to organizational and psychological pressures that impinge on personal flexibility. In-service training has played a critical role for both school professionals and lay participants.

At the same time, however, the principle of accountability implies a degree of countervailing power on the part of parents, pupils, and other lay participants. In many cases, the existence of an "external" presence, whether state or federal government or simply public opinion, has facilitated the entry of lay participants and has reinforced their role. South Carolina, for example, has mandated parent-teacher advisory councils at each school site and has given them the function of assisting in the preparation of school annual reports with the license to write their own report if they deem it necessary (Winecoff, 1982). Or, at the federal level, the Experimental School Program has mandated "community" involvement in decisions governing the use of school funds (Jackson, 1981).

By and large the more successful efforts at citizen participation would appear to transcend adversarial relationships among various school "interests." Not only are the resources for participation available, but the focus of participation goes beyond the "protection of interests." That some instances of successful participation of this type exist is testimony to the democratic credo that more participation is better participation. That this quality of participation is not the norm is testimony to some of the more intractable, systemic obstacles that must be confronted.

Citizen Participation and Equality

The effort to enhance political equality through citizen participation also has its roots in democratic values; yet, judged by this norm, the record of citizen participation may be even less successful. The citizen participation movement, in short, has not reduced political inequality to any significant degree.

Not only does the general literature on political participation reveal a consistent tendency for higher socio-economic groups to dominate political activism (Verba and Nie, 1972; Milbrath and Goel, 1977) but empirical studies of community organizations find strong socio-economic biases. For example, the major study of citizen participation in education initiated by the National Institute of Education found that the more effective citizen organizations were those populated by middle-income groups, while lower-income groups, often mandated by higher levels of government and funded externally, spent more time on organization maintenance and constituent service than on policy advocacy. The principal obstacles to policy effectiveness were the lack of resources necessary to sustain involvement over time and the absence of an informal, middle-class network with decision makers (Gittell, 1979).
network with decision makers (Gittell, 1979).

One of the most radical efforts at citizen participation—the community control movement in the New York City schools in 1966-68—evolved from the exasperation of minority groups with their inability to gain any significant school integration from an unresponsive school bureaucracy. As a result, minority parents demanded, under threat of boycott, that major school policy decisions regarding personnel, budget, and curriculum be placed directly in the hands of the local community. Because of its radical nature, the community control movement triggered a citywide strike by the teachers union and eventual legislation that replaced community control with a watered-down school decentralization scheme.

The "failure" of the community control movement provides useful insights into the reasons for limited success in citizen participation efforts generally. First, it is important to recognize that the community control movement represented an instantaneous, radically democratic effort to change the existing decision-making process. As such, it reflected a separatist route to empowerment rather than an integrative approach. As Barbara Hatton has observed (1977), the former aims at changes in the prevailing power structure that directly enhance the power status of particular groups, while the latter tries to integrate the disenfranchised into the prevailing power structure.

Each approach to empowerment reflects a distinct view of the prevailing power structure. By and large, the integrative approach is consistent with the pluralist view of power in American politics. In effect, decision making is viewed as open to new challenges to the status quo and based on competitive interaction among affected interests. The separatist approach to empowerment, in turn, reflects an elitist or neo-elitist view of the prevailing power structure. In this view, out-groups are obstructed in their efforts to influence policy by the "mobilization of bias" inherent in mainstream organizations. Institutionalization, in short, mobilizes prevailing values, beliefs, and goals in a manner that tends to exclude those not perceived as legitimate. Racial, ethnic, sex, and particularly class characteristics are often the visible symbols of legitimate or illegitimate claims on the policy process.

In addition, the community control, or separatist, approach to educational decision making rested on two related premises. First, it viewed efforts at integration as co-optive and therefore self-defeating. In short, a standardized, integrated public school system would be experienced by low-income minority children as inherently alien, with two possible outcomes: most children would fail to find learning meaningful in any way, thus falling farther and farther behind normal levels until the need to preserve some self-esteem would lead them to reject school; a few children would be able to make sufficient gains to given them hope of future success. The former group would become severely alienated from public schooling and the mainstream world it represents and thus would remain segregated as "failures"; the latter few would reject important aspects of their culture and personalities and would become personally alienated.

Because of its separatism, the community control movement was soundly criticized by liberals for isolating needy out-groups from mainstream educational and occupational opportunities, as well as deviating from the norms of due process and impartiality in both the learning and decision-making process. In part, the community control movement rationalized these shortcomings by pointing at flaws in the integrative approach. In addition, however, it rested on the democratic belief in the educational nature of participation and its corollary: that education, or real learning, must be participatory; that is, it must engage the subjective world of the learner. Because community control advocates saw mainstream schooling as inherently unresponsive, they sought a structure within which they could tailor learning to the subjective world of their children.

In light of the short-lived community control movement, one might draw two lessons for the basic democratic challenge mounted by the broader citizen participation movement. First, time is a critical ingredient; not only might changes be instituted more gradually than was done in the New York school system, but citizen participation should be given ample time to work. In fact, the essence of citizen participation is that it is a never-ending process. Indeed, the absence of definitive evidence demonstrating massive success in the citizen participation movement is not a reason for recoiling from these efforts. Instead, much more should be done. Furthermore, the evidence of limited success in terms of policy outcomes may mask more fundamental changes in the attitudes and skills of those who have been engaged in the citizen participation movement. Thus some effects may not show up in traditional, time-bound social science research.

The community control movement carries a second and very significant lesson. One reason it failed may be that it contained

the critical ingredient for success in empowering out-groups—
real, meaningful participation. Whether or not the New York
experiment allocated the most appropriate decision areas to
parents, it did give parents real decision-making power over
areas that were important to them. As such, it recognized the
importance of subjectivity in the decision-making process; what
parents felt was important was given tangible recognition and
release. Accordingly, the community control movement avoided
the many forms of what Sherry Arnstein (1964) has called manipulative or token participation. From a participatory perspective, parent advisory councils, public hearings, administrative
consultation, and the like are doomed to failure; most parents
and clients will see them as a waste of time (just as many of
their children will see their schooling experience as a waste of
time) and will remain alienated from the political process.

In sum, the citizen participation movement rests on a democratic ideology that poses a fundamental challenge to the
technocratic model of decision making. One need only reflect
on the discomfort most school administrators and teaching
professionals felt toward the community control movement to
appreciate the degree to which it posed a radical departure from
technocracy.

While the remainder of this chapter deals with alternative
mechanisms for balancing strains between democratic and
technocratic decision making, it is my contention that the citizen participation movement, to the degree that it is democratic,
reflects a qualitatively different vision from that underlying the
technocratic model. The latter reflects a faith in progress through
the impersonal mechanisms of technology, rational organization, and market capitalism. The former reflects a faith in the
improvability of human beings through active participation in
a life in common with others.[7]

THE NEW FEDERALISM

The Reagan Administration's approach to educational policy
contains three primary thrusts: (1) a shift from categorical federal grants (often targeted at needy populations) to block grants
to states for more general distribution, (2) an effort to reduce

federal red tape through deregulation of educational policies linked to federal monies, and (3) an inclination to enhance parent choice by providing aid in some manner for private education.

Underlying these three components is a mixture of objectives. Block grants are supposed to bring decisions regarding the use of revenues closer to the affected publics. States will have greater leeway to decide on the distribution of funds, and those, like Pennsylvania, that are attempting to follow the block grant model will shift greater responsibility to localities. This effort is tied in with the emphasis on deregulation—an effort to make educational spending more efficient by reducing the administrative personnel needed to apply for federal grants and to manage mandated programs.

In addition, the Reagan administration has displayed libertarian tendencies in advocating tuition tax credits for parents sending their children to private schools. Educational vouchers have also been prominent in education policy discussions. Either policy approach would attempt to provide individual consumers of education greater latitude in selecting schools. Both methods reflect a market philosophy aimed at the public school "monopoly."

How does the New Federalism "fit" on the efficiency-accountability and equality-liberty dimensions? While it is too early to tell in any definitive manner, it would seem that the Reagan approach represents a clear shift away from the goal of equality and a modest effort at increased efficiency couched in a manner that espouses greater accountability.

First, the Reagan policies manifestly shift resources in a manner that reduces revenue equality for schools. For example, the Administration's proposed FY83 budget contained a 38 percent reduction in funds for the compensatory Title I programs from their FY81 level, and a 34 percent reduction in comparable Title XX monies for day care. (On the other hand, the Head Start Program registered an 11 percent increase.) Similarly, monies for various targeted purposes placed in the block grant program were also reduced approximately 40 percent in a comparable time frame. Despite reduced revenues, the content of most liberal programs remains in place, thus requiring local schools to do the same job with fewer resources (when their clientele is arguably more needy).

Second, the administration's emphasis on block grants will, according to several analyses (*Education Week*, March 24, 1982), result in a redistribution of revenues away from urban, desegregating districts to those with sparser populations, and from public to private schools—not exactly a move in the direction of equality. In combination with deregulation, the shift from categorical to block grants is also likely to shift the distribution of funds within school districts. As Levy et al. have documented (1974), federal monies have tended to have a modestly redistributive impact in urban school systems, while state monies have not.

Finally, because states differ in their resources and policy priorities, the New Federalism is likely to result in regional inequities and substantial variations in the treatment of needy populations. In addition, many states face their own taxpayers' revolts and thus a squeeze on revenues from both above and below. In Massachusetts, for example, despite evidence that supporters of the tax-limiting Proposition 2 1/2 were in part demanding a more equitable system of taxation, the resulting cutbacks in school spending have been most pronounced in urban areas populated by large numbers of minority and lower working class pupils (Morgan, 1981, 1982a). Educational equality has suffered in two respects. Districts sending fewer graduates to four-year colleges and universities were likely to make greater reductions in their institutional budgets, and educational spending is likely to become more strongly associated with local property wealth. Similar trends seem likely in states like Michigan, Idaho, and California where voters have restricted funds for education. In addition, the shift away from educational equality seems to be evident in the area of integration, as challenges have been mounted to state authority to mandate desegregation in California and Illinois.

In regard to the efficiency-accountability dimension, the New Federalism is more ambiguous. In large part this is because efficiency is defined in terms of "what the public wants" using the market model. The New Federalism claims to be efficient in two respects. First, by "deregulating" public education (removing federal "strings"), the Reagan administration asserts that it is reducing federal requirements that have often taken attention away from the central educating task of schools and that have added an administrative layer to school systems. Second, by strengthening individual consumer choice, policies such as tuition tax credits and vouchers will streamline the delivery of educational services by making the product and its cost more accountable to consumers. Accountability is also enhanced by bringing decisions "closer" to affected publics (that is, shifting them from Washington to state capitals and local school districts).

In terms of its actual impact, it is not clear that the New Federalism will in fact enhance either efficiency or accountability. One reason is that the results still lie down the road, as does further Reagan administration action in the area of educational policy. If, however, the existing functions of federal aid to education are retained, as they seem likely to be, with reducing funding it may well be that efficiency will suffer. As David Cohen has argued, rather than liberating local school districts from externally imposed restrictions, the New Federalism will leave in place local organizational fragmentation and interest group activity. Ultimately, local school officials will have more problems with fewer resources (Cohen, 1982). This inefficiency will persist as long as equality is retained as a goal.

At the same time, there are signs that accountability will also suffer, at least in the short run. First, many of the fiscally pressed states and local school districts are engaged in "crisis planning" with the result that budget decisions are less accessible to public input than is normally the case (Impact 2 1/2, 1982). Second, the New Federalism is likely to result in reduced federal mandates for citizen participation in state and local decision making.

One reason liberals have such difficulty with the New Federalism is that it tends to define efficiency in a manner that is accountable to the claims of those who are more powerful at the state and local level, while liberals have tended to advocate policies that favor economically needy constituencies with relatively greater clout at the federal level. Liberals would counter the New Federalism by claiming that the most efficient way to provide revenue for needy populations is to target it in a manner that cannot be redirected through "something-for-everyone" formulae at the state level. Studies of the implementation of Great Society programs, for example, suggest that tighter rather than looser strings are needed if redistributive objectives are to be met (Pressman and Wildavsky, 1973). Thus it would appear that the crucial debate between liberals and conservatives is one of equality versus liberty, not efficiency versus accountability.

One may argue that the Reagan administration, like its predecessors, has devised a policy approach that rewards its more central constituencies while appealing to general public dissatisfaction with existing public services and their costs. By shifting greater responsibilities to the state and local level, the New Federalism taps into public sentiment that something has been lost in the general accountability of the public sector. However, there is little evidence that the New Federalism will in fact enhance citizen participation in education or any other area.

As a result, one cannot say that the New Federalism poses a democratic challenge to technocratic decision making. Instead of replacing expert decision makers with citizens, the New Federalism would appear merely to change the experts who make key policy and administrative decisions. State and local interest groups will play a greater role in policy formulation, while federal interest groups will play a diminished role, only because the arena of some decisions has been changed. The most democratic thrust of these proposals, educational vouchers, may threaten existing public school officials but will reward instead enterprising and efficient private (and public) officials. Real consumer accountability is likely to be no stronger than is currently the case in the private sector generally—a debatable point.

The only hedge on this bet is that needy federal policy constituencies will be energized by cutbacks to focus their attention on state and local politics. With this potential for increased political activism, there is an outside chance that the New Federalism will enhance the objectives of citizen participation.

DEMOCRACY AND TECHNOCRACY:
EDUCATIONAL POLICY CHOICES AND
PARADOXES

There can be little doubt that public policy in general and educational policy in particular are in a period of transition—buffeted by declining public confidence and shifting away from unquestioning acceptance of prevailing policy approaches with little clear vision of which direction will be taken in the years to come. On the one hand, one can detect a drift in the direction of smaller units of decision making—a drift that appeals to those on both the right and left who decry the decline of community. On the other hand, one can point to increasing global interdependence in economic, technological, and political terms.

We do not really know whether smaller-scale decision-making units will, in fact, increase public participation. Conclusions about participation will probably vary according to who participates, or, more accurately, whom one wishes to see participate more.

In essence, policymakers and their constituents face a basic policy choice and enduring policy paradoxes. First we must ask whether we will pursue the objective of educational equality more (or less) than we have done in past years. To answer in the negative is to accept the existence of what is rapidly becoming a permanent underclass in American cities—an explosive and oppressed group made up disproportionately of racial minorities. Put somewhat differently, to choose other public values (for example, less government intervention, at whatever level) is to count these as more critical than equality. The Reagan New Federalism, despite some of its rhetorical flourishes, appears to accept this condition, at least in the Northeast and Midwest. Thus far, the fiscally strapped states of these regions have shown little inclination or ability to generate revenues to revitalize the cities, and the prognosis for future tendencies in this direction is not good (Bahl, 1981).

To the degree that educational equality is given prominence in policy decisions, the question remains: how should we seek to enhance equality—through technocratic or democratic means or some combination of the two? Much of the prevailing dissatisfaction with public services would seem to indicate the need for greater emphasis on citizen participation in educational decision making, but this conclusion still contains two paradoxes.

First, there is the danger of self-defeating "manipulative" or "token" forms of public participation—in effect, gestures toward citizen participation that render them meaningless (in the eyes of the lay public) and thus reinforce nonparticipation. The answer suggested by the community control movement would seem to be devolution of educational decision making to small-scale units that include substantial numbers of affected clients. However, this answer, in turn, raises the short-term costs of separatist policies. The answer to this dilemma may be to opt for long-term gains, an approach that is not well suited to the traditional electoral process.

The egalitarian answer to problems raised by devolution generally points to a redistributive role on the part of the federal government—in particular, policies through which the federal government redistributes income and economic resources, stimulates the revitalization of urban areas through targeted aid of one type or another, and mandates certain protections of lower-income out-groups. The problem is that these policies again place significant emphasis on centralization, not devolution, of power. If one believes the maxim that control follows the dollar, the local decision-making units would not have sufficient real power to make participation seem worthwhile; hence we would once again face the liberal welfare state that seems to discourage widespread participation.

Two distinct approaches might be taken in attempting to force a new educational policy. One, following some of the initiatives of the Reagan administration, might be to disentangle federal and state/local policy roles by policy area. In other words, one might allocate nearly all responsibility for educational policy decisions and revenues to states and localities, while the federal government takes over near-total responsibility for economic welfare policies. Such an approach would have the advantage of increasing local decision-making leverage in education while retaining fundamental redistributive policies in the more effective federal hands.

In the interest of equality and citizen participation, however, such a shift would seem to require three qualifications. First, the level of federal efforts to enhance equality would have to be far greater than that proposed by the Reagan administration. Income redistribution would need to reflect a level that would facilitate the empowerment of out-groups; the federal government would also need to provide revenues for community organizing and for the revitalization of urban areas. Second, the federal government would need to play a continuing role in protecting basic educational rights of all pupils and would need to target significant revenues for programs such as Head Start. Finally, federal mandates for citizen participation at the local level might have to accompany federal revenues. In effect, we are back from where we started prior to the recent conservative shift.

A second and more radical approach would be to downplay the role of states entirely, opting instead for more of a bilevel governmental structure not unlike that found on a smaller scale in greater London. A federal-local (and even neighborhood) government partnership would seem to facilitate the twin objectives of equality and participation more effectively than the multigovernment federal system that currently prevails. Evidence of the effectiveness of such an approach can be seen in the federal Experimental Schools and Urban/Rural Development programs (Jackson, 1981) and the original Community Action Program. Such an approach would not eliminate the need for a state and municipal-level presence in educational policy, in part because it would encounter stiff resistance from organized interests at these levels and because some policy decisions (for example, collective bargaining or teacher certification) might be best handled at these levels.

In such a scheme, the federal emphasis would include two primary functions: (1) revenue redistribution and (2) maintenance of procedural safeguards. The former would arguably include ample income redistribution, revenue provision for community organization and community development, and redistribution of general educational funds. The latter would include the protection of basic educational rights and mandated procedural safeguards to ensure decision-making access to all sectors of the public.

A local emphasis would include two main components: (1) restructuring of decision making to distribute access to more citizens (including those who are effectively disenfranchised) and (2) increasing the role of lay citizens in significant policy decisions. In each case, it is possible to strike a more democratic or more technocratic balance. The latter might include electoral reform to ensure representation of subunits in centralized (for example, municipal-level) decision making and the incorporation of subjective client evaluations in assessing personnel performance and in developing budget priorities. The more democratic options would be to devolve significant decision making to submunicipal or neighborhood-school units and to include lay citizens, teachers, and administrators in decisions regarding curriculum, budget, and personnel.

It becomes readily apparent that neither policy option avoids the technocratic-democratic tensions between centralization-localism and expert-citizen control. These are, in fact, unavoidable tensions, for they are enduring paradoxes of educational policy, of democratic societies, and of politics generally. However, the direction one advocates for future policies would seem to reflect the degree to which one has greater faith in the effectiveness of universal, rational organization or in the power of lay citizens to become increasingly effective in self-government. The current evidence of cynicism, alienation, and various forms of unrest would seem to suggest the need for more of the latter.

NOTES

1. For an elaboration of this view, see Morgan, 1982b.

2. Lowery and Sigelman (1981) discuss the "political disaffection" explanation of the taxpayers' revolt but note that it has not been adequately tested. There is evidence that the passage of tax-limiting referenda is linked to a perception of "waste and corruption" in government, though not to the quality of public services per se (Ladd and Wilson, 1981; Patterson et al., 1980).

3. These findings, and those of other studies, can be interpreted in different ways depending on one's criteria for democracy (see Lutz and Iannaccone, 1978, for three alternative views).

4. For an argument that organizational unresponsiveness reflects more than bureaucratization, see Cohen (1982).

5. These are conveniently recorded in the publications of the Institute for Responsive Education in Boston. See especially, the survey of state actions (Clasby, 1979) and the IRE newsletter "Citizen Action in Education."

6. See the discussion in Jackson (1981) and studies such as Rutter et al., (1979) and Edmonds and Fredericksen (1978).

7. For a discussion of these two "visions," see the author's "Democratic Citizenship: An Evolving Post-Modern Paradigm," unpublished manuscript.

REFERENCES

Arnstein, Sherry 1969
"A Ladder of Citizen Participation," *American Institute of Planners Journal* 35:216–24.

Bahl, Roy, ed. 1981
Urban Government Finance: Emerging Trends. (Beverly Hills, Calif.: Sage Publications).

Clasby, Mirian 1979
"State Legislation for Citizen Participation Survey," in Don Davies et al., *Federal and State Impact on Citizen Participation in the Schools.*

Cohen, David K. 1982
"Policy and Organization: The Impact of State and Federal Educational Policy on School Governance," *Harvard Educational Review* 52:4:474–99.

Cronin, Joseph M. 1973
The Control of Urban Schools. (New York: The Free Press).

Davies, Don., et al. 1979
Federal and State Impact on Citizen Participation in the Schools. (Boston: Institute for Responsive Education).

Edmonds, Ron R., and J. R. Fredericksen 1978
Search for Effective Schools: The Identification and Analysis of City Schools That Are Instructionally Effective for Poor Children. (Cambridge, Mass.: Harvard University Center for Urban Studies).

Education Week 1981–82
Various issues, Marion, Ohio.

Gallup, George H. 1980
"The Twelfth Annual Gallup Poll of the Public's Attitudes Toward the Public Schools," *Phi Delta Kappan*, September, pp. 33–46.

Gittell, Marilyn, et al. 1979
    Citizen Organizations: Citizen Participation in Educational Decision-making. (Boston: Institute for Responsive Education).
Hatton, Barbara R. 1977
    "Schools and Black Community Development: A Reassessment of Community Control," *Education and Urban Society* 9:215–33.
Impact 2 1/2 (a university collaborative), Massachusetts Institute of Technology 1982
    Impact 2 1/2 January 15 and February 15.
Jackson, Barbara L. 1981
    "Federal Intervention and New Governance Structures," *Citizen Action in Education* 8:2:6–7.
Katz, Michael B. 1971
    Class Bureaucracy and the Schools. (New York: Praeger).
Ladd, Helen F., and Julie Boatright Wilson 1981
    "Proposition 2 1/2: Explaining the Vote." (Cambridge, Mass.: John F. Kennedy School of Government, Research Report R81–1, April).
Levy, Frank S., Arnold J. Meltsner, and Aaron Wildavsky 1974
    Urban Outcomes. (Berkeley: University of California Press).
Lowery, David, and Lee Sigelman 1981
    "Understanding the Tax Revolt: Eight Explanations," *American Political Science Review* 75:963–74.
Lutz, Frank W., and Laurence Iannaccone 1978
    Public Participation in Local School Districts. (Lexington, Mass.: Lexington Books).
Milbrath, Lester W., and M. L. Goel 1977
    Political Participation. 2d ed. (Chicago: Rand McNally).
Moore, Donald R., and Sharon Weitzman 1981
    "Advocacy: A Proven Method for Helping Children," *Citizen Action in Education* 8:2:1ff.
Morgan, Edward P. 1981
    "Public Preferences and Policy Realities: Proposition 2 1/2 in Massachusetts." Paper presented at the Northeastern Political Science Association meeting, Newark, N.J., November.
——— 1982a
    "The Effects of Proposition 2 1/2 in Massachusetts," *Phi Delta Kappan* 64:4:252–58.
——— 1982b
    "Two Paradigms of Urban Educational Policy: The Quest for Equality and its Central Dilemma, *Polity* 15:1:48–71.

Patterson, Franklin, Padraig O'Malley, and Raymond Torto 1980
   "University of Massachusetts Poll on Proposition 2 1/2." (Boston: Center for Studies in Policy and the Public Interest, May).
Pressman, Jeffrey L., and Aaron B. Wildavsky 1973
   Implementation. (Berkeley: University of California Press).
Rutter, Michael, et al. 1979
   Fifteen Thousand Hours: Secondary Schools and Their Effects on Children. (Cambridge: Harvard University Press).
Tucker, Harvey J., and L. Harmon Zeigler 1980
   Professionals versus the Public: Attitudes, Communication, and Response in School Districts. (New York: Longman).
Verba, Sidney, and Norman H. Nie 1972
   Participation in America: Political Democracy and Social Equality. (New York: Harper and Row).
Winecoff, Sandra Z. 1982
   "Citizen Participation in Developing an Effective School," *Citizen Action in Education* 9:2:1ff.

Part III

THE FUTURE OF PUBLIC DECISION MAKING IN THE UNITED STATES

10

Toward a Metapolicy for Social Planning

JACK DESARIO AND STUART LANGTON

The American character is marked by a passion for both democracy and expertise. As a people, we look to ourselves and experts for answers to our problems. In both, we harbor a deep abiding faith. We believe that through voting or direct participation citizens should have a say in decisions that affect their lives. We also have confidence that experts who are capable of putting a man on the moon or providing and improving the greatest array of consumer goods in the history of our civilization can offer us answers to some of our most complex public problems.

This is not to say that our civic faith in democracy and expertise has not been shaken from time to time. At times, our representative democracy has been polluted by excessive self-interest, greed, and apathy. Yet, periods of democratic reform and resurgence have followed. And the experts have not always been right. Their inventions or solutions have sometimes led to disaster or waste. Yet, improved inventions or refinements have usually followed technological mistakes. We still believe in progress.

The history of public policy making in Ameica has exhibited our faith in these two sources of authority in our society—the people and the experts. Our policy tradition has assumed a degree of compatibility between these sources of influence. We have assumed that the experts would offer choices in the best interest of the public and that the public would respect the findings of scientific experts. We have assumed that enlightenment and objectivity would prevail.

A GROWING INCOMPATIBILITY

During the past several decades, the assumed compatibility between the traditions of democratic participation and technological expertise has been called into question. As citizens have frequently become more polarized and adversarial in their politics and experts have often been bought by the highest bidder, the objectivity of both has been called into question. The result has been a growing distrust by many citizens of scientific experts and vice versa. As Duncan McRae, Jr., has observed:

Today, science and democracy symbolize alternative modes of guiding society. Until recently, they were widely believed to support one another; science enlightened the public and provided it with new alternatives, while democracy allowed science to flourish. But in recent years, the values of science and democracy have increasingly appeared to conflict, especially in their application to public choices. Insofar as public choices depend on expert information, science requires that this information be judged by experts rather than the electorate. Democracy, however, requires that the electorate have the ultimate power. Those who value democracy, or fear its erosion, sometimes see scientists as an elite serving special interests, or see applied science as simply unplanned and uncontrolled. (1973:228).

The advent of the technological era has forced technocracy and democracy to become intertwined in several ways. A review of these interactions illustrates the evolution of these current tensions. First, the technological revolution has enhanced the importance of technical knowledge and, therefore, the influence of expertise. Concurrently, however, Emmanuel Mesthene emphasizes that

[P]olitical requirements for our modern technological society call for a relatively greater public commitment on the part of individuals than in previous times. The reason for this, stated most generally, is that technological change has the effect of enhancing the importance of public decision making in society, because technology is continually creating new possibilities for social action as well as new problems that have to be dealt with. (1981:121)

Citizens are now becoming directly involved in greater numbers and with more issues than ever before. Even technological development policies, which were considered to be the sole purview of science in the past, have citizen representation. The inevitable result of this haphazard expansion and merger of citizen and expert participation has often been conflict and dissension. Based upon the distinct evolution of technocracy and democracy, representatives of each of these interests have fervently guarded their legitimacy with little understanding of the relative contributions of the other.

A second consequence of the technological society has been that technocracy as a process and array of procedures has pervaded almost all aspects of public planning. Experts, technical knowledge, and technical analytic methods constitute a part of the "technocratic" civic culture of government problem solving which citizens cannot avoid. These features of the new planning process can be used either to promote or frustrate citizen interests. Proper public education or familiarity with these tools can encourage citizens to conduct a systematic and accurate examination of their policy preferences. However, it has been found in many cases that these techniques have been used instead to confound and discourage citizen participation.

The third convergence represents an interesting paradox. The technological developments which provided the logic for the institutionalization of technocracy are now being hailed as promoting the technical capabilities essential to the expansion of participatory democracy. This perspective is based on observations of the social transformations produced by the technological revolution. It has generally been acknowledged that our society has shifted from an industrial to a postindustrial era. According to a growing number of social analysts, the postindustrial society can be more accurately referred to as the "information society" (Naisbitt, 1982; Masuda, 1980). This distinction is important because the information society is expected to produce a number of fundamental changes that may enhance citizen participation. Commenting on this pattern of development in the United States and Japan, Yoneji Masuda writes:

The information society will be a new type of human society, completely different from the present industrial society. . . . In the information society, computer technology will be the innovational technology that will constitute the developmental core, and its fundamental function will be to substitute for and amplify the mental labor of man. . . . In the information society, an information revolution resulting from development of the computer will rapidly expand information productive power, and make possible the mass production of cognitive, systematized information, technology, and knowledge. (1981:29, 31)

The growing importance of information is readily apparent in the United States. Now more than 60 percent of the workforce works with information. The diffusion of inexpensive electronics communications systems and personal computers has been phenomenal (Evans, 1979). It has been estimated that "from the beginning of time through 1980 there were only one million computers" (Naisbitt, 1982:25). According to Naisbitt, Commodore International, Ltd., one of many manufacturers of personal computers, expected to match the one million figure in 1982 sales alone.

The informational economy has profound implications for cultural, workplace, and residential change which may further strengthen opportunities for citizen participation. Decentralized information networks are replacing the factory as our societal symbol. The decline of heavy industry has "neutralized the pressure to centralize" (Naisbitt, 1982:99). In fact, general trends toward decentralization are becoming discernible. Without mass industrialization and the concentration of population it requires, more Americans are moving to small towns and cities. The large monolithic political structures required to guide the mass society are losing prominence. Local and regional decision making, in contrast, have been gaining in stature. "It is the smaller political units—cities, counties, and individual communities—that are claiming local authority over, and taking responsibility for, social issues that hit hard at the local level" (Naisbitt, 1982:102). These developments represent renewed opportunities for citizen participation. Citizen input is easier to achieve at the local level because of cost, familiarity, interest, access, and lack of bureaucratic complexity.

The information epoch is also viewed as providing a direct link between citizens and their decision making process. It is claimed that

[t]he technical difficulties that, until now have made it impossible for large numbers of citizens to participate in policy-making, have been solved by the revolution in computer-communications technology. . . . The development of communications satellites in particular, and home computers, along with the time-sharing system, together offer a solution to the problems of personnel, time, and costs. (Masuda, 1981:103)

The optimism generated by these new technical capabilities has led many futurists to question the wisdom and/or necessity of representational democracy. We are repeatedly told that participatory democracy is the political system of the future. Evans best represents this trend of thought when commenting on the problems of representational democracy:

This process was less glaringly inefficient in the days when information exchange itself was slow and laborious. But in the era of cheap, instant electronic communication, and particularly of cheap instant data processing, these turgid mechanisms are no longer justifiable. . . . One might even question the need for professional politicians who only act as the intermediary between the voter and the government system. (1979:216).

New communication devices do provide citizens with the opportunity to know just as much about the issues and just as rapidly. However, do these technical accomplishments justify the unequivocal claims for participatory democracy? Should citizens be involved in all issues? These questions bring us back to the original tensions between technocracy and democracy. It is obvious that in many situations we may desire, or even prefer, expert opinion (Morgan, 1978; Sapolsky, 1968). This realization suggests that the real issue which must be confronted is the appropriate interaction between these models.

Historically, public policy making has attempted simultaneously to "maximize" the contributions of citizens and experts. Technocracy and democracy were treated as separate and distinct sources of influence. Our experience and analyses of their social convergence indicate the shortcomings of this approach. Some of the most obvious failures of planning have resulted from the merger of these concepts under the banner of "maximization." In the absence of clearly defined roles or goals, citizens and experts have become engaged in conflict and confusion by operating out of each of their paradigms without accommodating the other. There are ideologial and practical tensions, contradictions, and incompatibilities between these approaches that make it impractical to "maximize" both ideals. The democratic ethos must adapt to options offered by objective scientific inquiry, and experts must respect the fears, desires, and preferences of the people.

TOWARD A METAPOLICY FOR SOCIAL PLANNING

The notion of convergence illustrates the host of new issues and problems that have emerged as a result of our attempts to harness the traditions and forces of technocracy and democracy. The difficulties we have experienced in our attempts to maximize these models raise many important normative questions for our society. Problems of interaction suggest that we must determine the planning values we wish to promote within various policy contexts, or we will continue the current pattern of frustration and failure. This consequence makes it essential to devise theoretical frameworks and concepts to inform a "metapolicy" for the future. Metapolicy, defined as a "policy on how to make policy," would be expected to specify the most appropriate methods of reaching public decisions (Dror, 1971:74). Within this context, metapolicy would have to identify the relative, optimal contributions of citizens and experts. This determination will have a profound impact upon the issues of effectiveness, rationality, responsiveness, and efficacy.

Before actual decision making methods that reflect a meta-policy can be suggested, a number of critical questions must be resolved:

1. What is the proper interaction between technocracy and democracy?
2. What types of policy considerations or issues are most appropriate to citizen versus technocratic decision making?
3. What are some of the procedures and methods that facilitate citizen versus expert participation?

The most fundamental issue to the development of effective metapolicy is the identification of the appropriate roles of citizens versus experts. A number of criteria must be developed and applied to policy decisions to help us clarify these contributions. Clearly, the need for and desirability of citizen and expert involvement varies a great deal across social programs. Therefore, the "type of decision" to be made is an important initial determinant of the relative role of each group.

As a framework for developing a metapolicy, we would concur with Kantrowitz (1975) that policy considerations involve three issues: technical decisions, value decisions, and mixed decisions. When viewed in this way, policymakers, scientific experts, and concerned citizens can better appreciate the unique resources each group can bring to each of these three types of decisions.

Technical Decisions

Technical decisions are those that are based solely on the application and extrapolation of scientific issues. They are usually phrased as "what is" or factual questions. What is the best way to explode a bomb to attain the highest force of explosion? What is the best way to propel a capsule to the moon? Are particular pharmaceuticals carcinogenic? Policy issues which are purely technical considerations should remain essentially the domain of experts. Scientists at the Food and Drug Administration, for example, are best qualified to determine whether food substances comply with particular standards or regulations. The public accountability of experts is limited to evaluations of the professionalism of their actions.

Value Decisions

Value decisions are those that are concerned solely with the resolution of important normative or societal issues. Generally they involve issues of social behavior and do not require a commitment of social expenditures or resources. They are best referred to as moral "what should be" questions. Should we pass a constitutional amendment banning abortion? Should school prayer be made mandatory? Opinions on these issues are not derived from empirical analysis or rational deduction; rather they reflect the social dispositions of the society. Given the features of value decisions, citizens are viewed as best qualified to resolve disputes over these societal goals and directions.

Mixed Decisions

The mixed decision has become increasingly prevalent as a result of our technological society. These decisions represent issues that have both a technical and value component. The dual nature of these policies makes them the most complex to resolve. Should experts or citizens be entrusted with final authority? Why? Important mixed decisions have been the source of great social antagonism due to the lack of a well-defined process which logically specifies the appropriate planning contributions of each group. Decisions as to whether we should construct the SST, develop nuclear power plants, regulate air pollution, install mandatory auto safety restraints, or purchase CAT scanners have significant technical and value considerations. Mixed decisions are also important because they are usually associated with significant allocations of funds and resources.

The demands of mixed decisions require joint participation by citizens and experts. Multistage decision-making processes can be devised to optimize the appropriate contributions of each of these groups. The logic of this process is derived from the premise that it is possible to separate the normative and technical elements of a mixed decision (Collingridge, 1980; Kantrowitz, 1975; Task Force of the Presidential Advisory Group on Anticipated Advances in Science and Technology, 1976). Kantrowitz provides the rationale for this separation when he argues:

It has occasionally been maintained that the scientific and nonscientific components are generally inseparable. It is, of course, true that a final political decision cannot be separated from scientific information on which it must be based. The reverse is not true; a scientific question which, logically, can be phrased as anticipating the results of an experiment can always be separated from any political considerations. Thus the question—Should we build a hydrogen bomb?—is not a purely scientific question. A related scientific question—Can we build a hydrogen bomb?—could in principle be answered by an experiment. (1975:506)

The first stage of mixed decision making is designed to attain scientific opinion on technical feasibility, social costs, and social implications.

This objectivity is complicated by the growing realization that the methods and theories of science do not produce a single "unambiguously correct answer" (Mazur, 1973:251). Conflicting interpretations of scientific data by experts have become highly publicized for technical issues such as nuclear energy, environmental disturbances to the ozone layer, and food additives (Task Force of the Presidential Advisory Group on Anticipated Advances in Science and Technology, 1976). As a result of these disputes, a wide array of new methods for presenting and formulating scientific opinion have been devised. Adversarial models are best applied to the requirements of mixed decision making (Mazur, 1973; Collingridge, 1980). In accord with this procedure, disagreeing experts present their cases before a panel of judges. This panel should consist of established experts in the area and citizen representatives. The exact composition of this panel is dictated by considerations detailed by the second stage of the planning process. The testimony, debate, and questioning engendered is expected to illustrate areas of scientific consensus and contention.

The first stage of planning provides expert analysis of technological capabilities, costs, and shortcomings; however, the problems of "sorting out value differences remain" (President's Commission for a National Agenda for the Eighties, 1980:73). The second stage of this process is responsible for the formulation of "informed" value articulation. Previously, we recognized the preeminence of citizens in resolving value decisions. Although citizens are expected to assume an imporant role during this second stage, the demands and expectations placed upon them are vastly different. The nature of mixed decisions requires a close interaction between technical analysis and value articulation. Mixed decisions are not simply concerned with normative standards. These policies, in many cases, entail large allocations of limited resources for the achievement of social goals. Value articulation, for citizens involved in mixed decision making, requires the identification of social objectives, as dictated by social risks, costs, and capabilities.

The differing demands placed upon citizens by value versus mixed decisions dictate that distinct decision-making procedures must be utilized. Value decisions often may not involve as substantial amounts of time and energy. Everyone is equally capable and qualified to state their normative preferences. As a result, these types of decisions are conducive to mass participation mechanisms such as referenda. Nonetheless, citizens should recognize that the quality of the justification of their values often does demand considerable time and effort. There is a significant difference between "saying one's piece," or merely stating one's preference, and arguing thoughtfully and thoroughly for the values one is defending. In this respect, dedicated citizen advocates should be challenged to provide the same rigor in defending their values as they expect of scientific experts in defending their technical views. Merely to express public opinion, as Walter Lippman once observed, is not enough. What is more compelling is for the dedicated citizen to demonstrate the efficacy of their values and the logic of their conclusions.

Mixed decisions often make great time demands on citizen participants. Citizens must attend technical meetings, decipher scientific presentations and controversies, and logically resolve conflicting social desires and capabilities. Given these responsibilities and complexities, it is unrealistic to expect mass participation in carefully reviewing and revising policy options in regard to mixed decisions. What is required are smaller groups of highly motivated citizens. In creating such groups, policymakers are faced with the decision of how much authority they can grant to citizens. The major options, in this respect, are between the more traditional advisory committee model with limited citizen power and a citizen court model that grants a majority membership to citizens among a panel of judges with authority to make a decision. The limitation of the former model is the danger of citizens being co-opted or ignored (Arnstein, 1970). The danger of the latter model is that policymakers may have to live with a decision with which they are not happy. Whichever model is selected, it is critical that the citizen group be given the technical resources to assist them in addressing complex technical issues (Petersen, 1984).

A related procedural question for policymakers concerns the potential continuation of citizen involvement in monitoring policy implementation. Certainly, implementation issues will be delegated to professional bureaucracies for their consideration and design. However, because factual "what is" questions may emerge during this phase of the policy process, the continued involvement of citizens may continue to provide helpful contributions despite the potential uneasiness of bureaucrats (Delli Priscoli, 1982).

The tripartite framework for decision making identified above suggests specialized resources that concerned citizens and technological experts can bring to policy making. However, in advocating this model, we would not want to exclude the contributions that each can make to the other. Some citizens are indeed capable of addressing complex technical issues, and scientific experts should not forfeit their right to address value issues. In fact, in the interest of public policies that seek that ever-amorphous but important "public interest," we would propose that, when possible, citizens organize to become active participants in the review of technical decisions and that scientists organize to review normative considerations.

How might these things be done? To answer this question at a practical level, we would suggest the following. First, we would encourage any group of citizens engaged in policy efforts to organize a "technical review group." This group might consist of average laypersons and people with particular scientific expertise. The idea here is not to allow the technical contribution of "experts" to go unexamined. Second, we would encourage experts to form "value implication review groups." The purpose of these groups would be for experts to consider the normative consequences of their recommendations on society.

INSTITUTIONALIZATION OF METAPOLICY

The contributions of citizens versus experts may vary considerably depending on the nature of each policy consideration. Citizen influence may range from a position of policy dominance (value decisions) to one of minimal or noninvolvement (technical decisions). These variations indicate the importance of designing and/or identifying decision-making structures which can reflect desired contributions. Numerous approaches to policy participation have been instituted in the United States and other countries (Nelkin and Pollak, 1979; Nelkin, 1977). A review of these techniques suggests that they form a participational continuum (see Figure 10.1). Each strategy posits a slightly different role for citizens and experts. The right side of the continuum features processes which provide citizens with dominant and proactive roles, while the left side represents methods that restrict citizens to reactive or minimal involvement vis-à-vis experts. Consistent with this illustration, "initiatives" are viewed as most vigorously promoting citizen participation. Initiatives dictate that the policy agenda is to be determined and resolved by direct citizen action. "Professional commissions," in contrast, determine policy directives through technocratic debate and analysis. Experts from the public and private sectors are assembled to determine consensus. Citizen input, if it exists, is restricted to observation or commentary on the specific issues being debated. Strategies situated between these extremes represent some degree of compromise between experts and citizens. The further to the right they are located, the more they favor citizens.

The sheer diversity of the decision-making methods available for public planning does not guarantee success. Even after we

Figure 10.1
Participation Continuum of Decision-Making Techniques

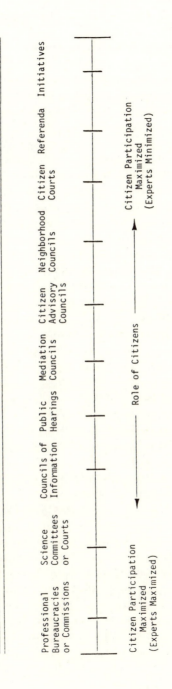

identify strategies which are consistent with desired values, the problems of implementation remain. Studies indicate that a considerable degree of variation exists in the quality of participation for any particular approach. Systematic comparative evaluation and experimentation is needed to specify the determinants of successful programs. Checkoway, O'Rourke, and Bulls' analysis (1984) provides a useful example of this type of research. These studies are essential to the development of decision-making structures of the future. This analytic void is most apparent in regard to citizen participation. Although we have experienced a number of successes, controversy still surrounds many fundamental questions of citizen involvement. Are government-mandated organizations less effective than self-initiated citizen organizations (Gittell, 1983; Rich, 1983)? What are the benefits of public education and orientation programs? Does the demographic composition of citizens matter? Are planning staffs needed? Do procedural reforms enhance participation?

The major premise of this book has been to challenge the separation between technocratic and democratic traditions in policy making and to advocate greater integration among experts and citizens in public policy solving and decision making. While this need grows in intensity, it is clear that our ability to manage the integration of expert and citizen contributions in policy making is quite modest. As James Petersen has observed: "Our problem is that technology continues to develop far more rapidly than 'participatory technology' " (1984:9). Nonetheless, as many of the essays above have illustrated, it is possible in many instances to achieve constructive integration of these dual sources of influence.

The great challenge for our society (and others as well) is how to continue to increase our ability to integrate effectively technocratic and democratic contributions in addressing complex technological issues. This challenge can be met most effectively by establishing a metapolicy, a policy about how to make policies, at each level of government and among respective branches and agencies. While the metapolicy of each unit or branch of government may differ, we would propose that the following five principles be recognized: (1) that the dangers associated with maximizing expert and citizen contributions without joint review and interpretation be avoided; (2) that the unique contributions of experts at the technical level and of citizens at the normative level of policy making be encouraged but that a later stage of mixed review be established that involves experts and citizens in examining issues of impact and trade-offs regarding technocratic and democratic considerations; (3) that the issue of the role and power of citizens be made explicit at the outset, and appropriate procedures be developed to reflect power-sharing arrangements; (4) that adequate information, and access to it, and financial and technical resources be made available to citizens; and (5) that government be experimental in selecting, evaluating, and refining procedures for integrating expert and citizen contributions that are most effective in dealing with the unique policy issues with which each is concerned.

It would be our hypothesis that principles such as these will have to be adopted as the number of complex technological policy issues increase for any governmental unit. The cost in conflict, frustration, expense, litigation, and time will be too great otherwise (Delli Priscoli, 1982). The critical choice of governmental units will be either to develop episodic and incremental responses to this challenge or to formulate a more systematic metapolicy. We propose the latter approach because it is easier to manage, more cost effective, and easier for all parties to understand.

When a game becomes more serious and has critical consequences in creating potential winners or losers, the rules of the game become more important. While players may challenge or want to change rules once they are established, the absence of rules may lead to still worse: refusal to play or attempts to destroy the game itself. As the public policy stakes regarding complex technological issues continue to increase, those who must manage the policy process must create rules for the appropriate involvement of citizens and experts. To fail to do this is to court unnecessary turmoil at best and potential policy disasters at worst.

REFERENCES

Arnstein, Sherry 1970
    "Eight Rungs on the Ladder of Citizen Participation," in Edgar

Cahn and Barry Passett, *Citizen Participation: A Casebook in Democracy*. (Trenton, N.J.: Community Action Training Institution).

Calder, Nigel 1969
Technopolis. (London, England: MacGibbon and Kee).

Checkoway, Barry, Thomas W. O'Rourke, and David Bull 1984
"Correlates of Consumer Participation in Health Planning Agencies: Findings and Implications from a National Survey," *Policy Studies Review* 3, 2.

Cole, Richard 1981
"Participation in Community Service Organizations," *Journal of Community Action* 1:53–60.

Collingridge, David 1980
The Social Control of Technology. (New York: St. Martin's Press).

Delli Priscoli, Jerry 1982
"The Enduring Myths of Public Involvement," *Citizen Participation*, 3:3–4.

Dror, Yehezkel 1971
Design for Policy Sciences. (New York: Elsevier).

Evans, Christopher 1979
The Micro Millennium. (New York: Viking Press).

Evashwick, Connie 1971
The Community Participation in Health Movement. (Boston: Harvard School of Public Health.

Gianos, Phillip 1974
"Scientists as Policy Advisors," *Western Political Quarterly* 27:429–56.

Gittell, Marilyn 1983
"The Consequences of Mandating Citizen Participation," *Policy Studies Review* 3,1:90–95.

Jones, Charles 1977
An Introduction to the Study of Public Policy, 2d ed. (North Scituate, Mass.: Duxbury Press).

Kantrowitz, Arthur 1975
"Controlling Technology Democratically," *American Scientist* 63:505–9.

Krause, Elliott 1968
"Functions of a Bureaucratic Society," *Social Problems* 15:129–43.

McCrae, Duncan, Jr. 1973
"Science and the Formation of Policy in a Democracy," *Minerva* 11:228–42.

Masuda, Yoneji 1980
The Information Society. (Tokyo, Japan: Institute for the Informative Society).

Mazur, Allan 1973
"Disputes Between Experts," *Minerva* 10:244–62.
Mesthene, Emmanuel 1981
"The Role of Technology in Society," in Albert Teich, ed., *Technology and Man's Future*, 3d ed. (New York: St. Martin's Press).
Morgan, Michael 1978
"Bad Science and Good Policy Analysis," *Science* 199:46–52.
Naisbitt, John 1982
Megatrends. (New York: Warner Books).
Nelkin, Dorothy 1977
Technological Decisions and Democracy. (Beverly Hills, Calif.: Sage Publications).
Nelkin, Dorothy, and Michael Pollack 1979
"Public Participation in Technological Decisions," *Technology Review* 81,8:55–64.
Petersen, James, ed. 1984
Citizen Participation in Science Policy. (Amherst: University of Massachusetts Press).
President's Commission for a National Agenda for the Eighties 1980
Science and Technology Promises and Dangers in the Eighties. (Washington, D.C.: Government Printing Office).
Rich, Richard 1983
"Balancing Autonomy and Capacity in Community Organizations," *Policy Studies Review* 3,1:96–101.
Sapolsky, Harold 1968
"Science Voters," *Science* 162:427–33.
Sclove, Richard 1982
"Decision Making in a Democracy," *The Bulletin of the Atomic Scientists* 38:44–48.
Task Force of the Presidential Advisory Group on Anticipated Advances in Science and Technology 1976
"The Science Court Experiment," *Science* 193:653–56.

Bibliography

Abrams, Nancy E., and Joe R. Primack. 1980.
  "The Public and Technological Decisions." *Bulletin of the Atomic Scientists* 36:6:44–48.
Arnstein, Sherry. 1969.
  "A Ladder of Citizen Participation." *American Institute of Planners Journal* 35:7:216–24.
Baker, David E. 1978.
  "State, Regional, and Local Experiments in Anticipatory Democracy: An Overview." In C. Bezold, ed., *Anticipatory Democracy, People in the Politics of the Future.* New York: Random House.
Bezold, Clement. 1977.
  Strengthening Citizen Access and Governmental Accountability. Washington, D.C.: Exploratory Project for Economic Alternatives.
———, ed. 1978.
  Anticipatory Democracy, People in the Politics of the Future. New York: Random House.
———. 1979.
  "Participation in Shaping the Future Alternative Futures for Citizen Education." *Futurics* 3:3:225–44.
Bireland, Donald, 1971.

"Community Action Boards and Maximum Feasible Participation." *American Journal of Public Health* 61:293.

Bratt, Rachel G. 1986.
"Public Housing: The Controversy and Contribution." In Rachel Bratt, Chester Hartman, and Martin Meyerson, eds., *Critical Perspectives on Housing*. Philadelphia Temple University Press.

———. 1986.
"Community-Based Housing Programs: Overview and Assessment." In Stuart Langton and James Petersen, eds., *Self-Help in America*. Lexington, Mass.: Lexington Books.

Calder, Nigel. 1969.
Technopolis. London, England: MacGibbon and Kee.

Caldwell, Lynton D., Lester Hayes, and Ian MacWhirter. 1976.
Citizens and the Environment. Bloomington: Indiana University Press.

Clasby, Mirian. 1979.
"State Legislation for Citizen Participation Survey." In Don Davies, *Federal and State Impact on Citizen Participation in the Schools*. Boston: Institute for Responsive Education.

Cobb, Roger, and Charles Elder. 1972.
Participation in American Politics: The Dynamics of Agenda-Building. Boston: Allyn and Bacon.

Collingridge, David. 1980.
The Social Control of Technology. New York: St. Martin's Press.

Cupps, D. Stephen. 1977.
"Emerging Problems of Citizen Participation." *Public Administration Review* 37:478–87.

Davies, Don. 1979.
Federal and State Impact on Citizen Participation in the Schools. Boston: Institute for Responsive Education.

Delbecq, Andre, and Andrew H. Van de Ven. 1982.
"A Group Process Model for Problem Identification and Program Planning." In Richard D. Bingham and Marcus E. Ethridge, eds., *Reaching Decisions in Public Policy and Administration*. New York: Longman.

DeSario, Jack. 1983.
"The Paradox of Health Planning." *Citizen Participation* 4:5:7–14.

DeSario, Jack, and Stuart Langton, eds. 1984.
Symposium on Citizen Participation and Public Policy. Symposium in *Policy Studies Review* 3:2:223–323.

Dunlap, Thomas. 1981.
DDT: Scientists, Citizens and Public Policy. Princeton, N.J.: Princeton University Press.

Ellul, Jacques. 1964.
    The Technological Society. New York: Vintage Books.
Evans, Christopher. 1979.
    The Micro Millennium. New York: Viking Press.
Fagence, Michael. 1977.
    Citizen Participation in Planning. New York: Pergamon Press.
Gittell, Marilyn. 1980.
    The Limits of Citizen Participation. Beverly Hills, Calif.: Sage Publications.
———. 1983.
    "The Consequences of Mandating Citizen Participation." *Policy Studies Review* 2:2:90–95.
Gittell, Marilyn, et al. 1979.
    Citizen Organizations: Citizen Participation in Educational Decisionmaking. Boston: Institute for Responsive Education.
Goodsell, Charles, ed. 1981.
    The Public Encounter When State and Citizen Meet. Bloomington: Indiana University Press.
Hatton, Barbara R. 1982.
    "Schools and Black Community Development: A Reassessment of Community Control." *Education and Urban Society* 9:215–33.
Kantrowitz, Arthur. 1975.
    "Controlling Technology Democratically." *American Scientist* 63:505–9.
Kweit, Mary Grisez, and Robert W. Kweit. 1981.
    Implementing Citizen Participation in a Bureaucratic Society. New York: Praeger Special Studies.
Langton, Stuart, ed. 1978.
    Citizen Participation in America. Lexington, Mass.: Lexington Books.
———. 1986.
    Self-Help in America. Lexington, Mass.: Lexington Books.
———. 1981.
    "Evolution of a Federal Citizen Involvement Policy." *Policy Studies Review* 1:369–78.
Lewis, Sherman. 1980.
    Reform and the Citizen. North Scituate, Mass.: Duxbury Press.
Lindblom, Charles E. 1977.
    Politics and Markets: The World's Political-Economic Systems. New York: Basic Books.
Lipsky, Michael. 1980.
    Street Level Bureaucracy Dilemmas of the Individual in Public Service. New York: Russell Sage Foundation.

Lowi, Theodore. 1979.
    The End of Liberalism: The Second Republic of the United States. 2d
    ed. New York: W. W. Norton.
Lutz, Frank W., and Laurence Iannaccone. 1978.
    Public Participation in Local School Districts. Lexington, Mass.:
    Lexington Books.
McCrae, Duncan, Jr. 1973.
    "Science and the Formation of Policy in a Democracy." *Minerva*
    11:228–42.
Mansbridge, Jane. 1980.
    Beyond Adversary Democracy. New York: Basic Books.
Masuda, Yoneji. 1980.
    The Information Society. Tokyo, Japan: Institute for the Informa-
    tive Society.
Mazmanian, David, and Jeanne Nienaber. 1979.
    *Can Organizations Change? Environmental Protection, Citizen Par-
    ticipation, and the Corps of Engineers.* Washington, D.C.: Brook-
    ings Institution.
Mazur, Allan. 1973.
    "Disputes Between Experts." *Minerva* 10:244–62.
Medin, Myron J. 1975.
    "Make Public Participation Produce Results." *American City and
    County* 90:104.
Milbrath, Lester W., and M. L. Goel. 1977.
    Political Participation. 2d ed. Chicago: Rand McNally.
Moore, Wilbert, ed. 1972.
    Technology and Social Change. Chicago: Quadrangle Books.
Morgan, Michael. 1978.
    "Bad Science and Good Policy Analysis," *Science* 199:46–52.
Mosher, Frederick. 1982.
    Democracy and the Public Service. New York: Oxford University
    Press.
Naisbitt, John. 1982.
    Megatrends. New York: Warner Books.
Nelkin, Dorothy, ed. 1977.
    Technological Decisions and Democracy. Beverly Hills, Calif.: Sage
    Publications.
Nelkin, Dorothy, and Michael Pollack. 1979.
    "Public Participation in Technological Decisions," *Technology
    Review* 81:55–64.
Olsen, Marvin. 1984.
    *Participatory Pluralism: Political Participation and Influence in the
    United States and Sweden.* Chicago: Nelson-Hall.

Paglin, Max, and Edgar Shor. 1977.
"Regulatory Agency Responses to the Development of Public Participation." *Public Administration Review* 37:140–48.

Pearlman, Janice. 1978.
"Grassroots Participation from Neighborhood to Nation." In Stuart Langton, ed., *Citizen Participation in America*. Lexington, Mass.: Lexington Books.

President's Commission for a National Agenda for the Eighties. 1980.
Science and Technology Promises and Dangers in the Eighties. Washington, D.C.: Government Printing Office.

Primack, Joel, and Frank von Hippel. 1974.
Advice and Dissent: Scientists in the Political Arena. New York: Basic Books.

Redford, Edward. 1969.
Democracy in the Administrative State. New York: Oxford University Press.

Rich, Richard C., and Walter A. Rosenbaum, eds. 1981.
Citizen Participation in Public Policy. Symposium in *Journal of Applied Behavioral Science* 17:4:439–614.

Rodale, Robert. 1981.
Our Next Frontier. Emmaus, Pa.: Rodale Press.

Rosenbaum, Nelson M. 1978.
"The Origins of Citizen Involvement in Federal Programs." In Clement Bezold, ed., *Anticipatory Democracy, People in the Politics of the Future*. New York: Random House.

Rosenbaum, Walter. 1977.
The Politics of Environmental Concern. 2d ed. New York: Praeger.
———. 1979.
"Public Participation: Required, But Is It Important?" *Citizen Participation* 1:1:12.

Schattschneider, E. E. 1960.
The Semi-Sovereign People. New York: Holt, Rinehart, and Winston.

Teich, Albert, ed. 1981.
Technology and Man's Future. New York: St. Martin's Press.

Toffler, Alvin. 1970.
Future Shock. New York: Random House.
———. 1980.
The Third Wave. New York: Morrow.

Tucker, Harvey J., and L. Harmon Zeigler. 1980.
Professionals versus the Public: Attitudes, Communications, and Response in School Districts. New York: Longman.

U.S. Advisory Commission on Intergovernmental Relations. 1979.
    Citizen Participation in the American Federal System. Report A-73.
    Washington, D.C.: ACIR.
Verba, Sidney, and Norman H. Nie. 1972.
    Participation in America: Political Democracy and Social Equality. New
    York: Harper and Row.
Vickers, Geoffrey. 1972.
    Freedom in a Rocking Boat: Changing Values in an Unstable Society.
    Middlesex, England: Penguin Books.
Weissberg, Robert. 1974.
    Political Learning, Political Choice and Democratic Citizenship. En-
    glewood Cliffs, N.J.: Prentice-Hall.
Winecoff, Sandra Z. 1982.
    "Citizen Participation in Developing an Effective School." *Citi-
    zen Action in Education* 9:2:1ff.
Winner, Langdon. 1977.
    *Autonomous Technology: Technics-Out-of-Control as a Theme in Po-
    litical Thought.* Cambridge, Mass.: MIT Press.

Index

About the Contributors

CLEMENT BEZOLD is the Executive Director of the Institute for Alternative Futures and President of Alternative Futures Associates. He is a political scientist who has worked and written extensively on the future of health care. Dr. Bezold is a consultant to governors and state legislators, hospital and pharmaceutical companies, and professional associations.

RACHEL G. BRATT is an Assistant Professor in the Department of Urban and Environmental Policy at Tufts University specializing in housing and community development. She is the co-editor of *Critical Perspectives on Housing*. Dr. Bratt received a Ph.D. from MIT and currently serves on the Multifamily Advisory Committee of the Massachusetts Housing Finance Agency and the Consumer Advisory Council of the Federal Reserve Bank.

JACK DESARIO is an Assistant Professor in the Department of Political Science at Case Western Reserve University. He has published essays in various books and journals on citizen participation and health policy.

MARCUS E. ETHRIDGE is an Associate Professor of Political Science at the University of Wisconsin–Milwaukee. His published research has emphasized the policy and representational implications of changes in bureaucratic structure and procedure.

VICTORIA LYNN FEDOR-THURMAN is currently employed by the Department of Social Services, County of Santa Clara, California. She is actively working on comparable worth issues, passage of the ERA, and toxic waste issues.

MARY GRISEZ KWEIT is a Professor of Political Science at the University of North Dakota. She received her Ph.D. from the University of Pennsylvania. Her publications have focused on political behavior with emphasis on citizen participation and party activism, and she is currently working on a book on participation in urban politics.

ROBERT W. KWEIT is a Professor of Political Science and Director of the Master of Public Administration program at the University of North Dakota. He received his Ph.D. from the University of Pennsylvania in 1974. He has presented papers and published in the areas of citizen participation, policy analysis, and the bureaucracy, and is currently working on a book on participation in urban politics.

STUART LANGTON is Lincoln Filene Professor of Citizenship and Public Administration at Tufts University and is Executive Director of the Lincoln Filene Center for Citizenship and Public Administration. He has served as consultant to over 100 government agencies and non-profit organizations. He is currently the editor of *Citizen Participation Magazine* and has edited several books in the field of citizen participation.

EDWARD P. MORGAN is currently an Associate Professor in the Government Department at Lehigh University. Professor Morgan has published a number of works focusing on the interplay between politics and education.

JAMES C. PETERSEN is an Associate Professor of Sociology at Western Michigan University. A specialist in organizational and political sociology, he has conducted research on organizational politics, science-related social conflicts, and public participation in policy formation. His publications include two edited books.

MICHAEL D. REAGAN is Professor of Political Science at the University of California, Riverside, and the author of *The Managed Economy* and *The New Federalism*.

THOMAS L. VAN VALEY is the Director of the Kercher Center for Social Research at Western Michigan University and a Professor in the Department of Sociology. His current works include studies of the origin and mobility of sociology department chairs and the impact of the computer on society.